*The Cherokee Nation
in the Civil War*

The Cherokee Nation in the Civil War

CLARISSA W. CONFER

University of Oklahoma Press : Norman

Library of Congress Cataloging-in-Publication Data

Confer, Clarissa W., 1965–
     The Cherokee nation in the Civil War / Clarissa W. Confer.
          p.   cm.
     Includes bibliographical references and index.
     ISBN 0-8061-3803-3 (alk. paper).
     ISBN 978-0-8061-3803-9
     1. Cherokee Indians—Wars. 2. Indians of North America—History—
Civil War, 1861–1865. 3. United States—History—Civil War, 1861–1865—
Participation, Indian. I.Title.

     E99.C5.C713 2007
     973.089'97557—dc22

                                                        2006025549

The paper in this book meets the guidelines for permanence and durability of the Committee on Production Guidelines for Book Longevity of the Council on Library Resources, Inc. ∞

1   2   3   4   5   6   7   8   9   10

For John, who always knows I can do it

Contents

Illustrations

FIGURES

MAPS

Acknowledgments

Over the course of this work I have accumulated debts for assistance and kindness both at numerous research institutions and at home. The professionalism of John Lovett and the staff of the Western History Collections, University of Oklahoma, contributed enormously to my work. The excellent facilities and efficient operation of the archives under Sarah Erwin of the Thomas Gilcrease Institute of American History and Art provided ideal conditions for productive research. Bill Welge and the overworked staff at the Indian Archives of the Oklahoma Historical Society took time from their busy schedules to help in every way and welcomed me into their basement for a summer.

I would like to thank Gary Gallagher for expanding the horizons of Civil War studies to include American Indians. Thanks to Theda Perdue for the warmth and generosity she brought to the scholarly pursuit of Indian history. John Frantz provided what every young instructor needs to guide her career: a role model of commitment and concern for students.

On the home front, I owe a great debt to my parents. Without their moral, financial, and spiritual support this treatise would never have been written. They gave their children the greatest gift of all—the freedom to be whomever they chose. Finally, unending gratitude to my constant companions Teton and John. One lay at my feet for countless hours of reading and writing and provided an excuse to ponder difficult questions on long walks. The other provided endless support and encouragement and enriched me with a faith in my abilities that far surpassed my own. We have been together in this enterprise from the first day unto the last.

*The Cherokee Nation
in the Civil War*

Introduction

I want to write the history of the Cherokee Nation as it should be written, not as white men will write it and as they will tell the tale, to screen and justify themselves.

JOHN ROLLIN RIDGE

The American Civil War remains the deadliest conflict in American history. Americans in every region grappled with the pervasive impact of the war, which even affected areas considered marginal to mainstream politics and society. Countless stories of wartime death, dislocation, and destruction testified to the terrible situation in Indian Territory, the location of the western Cherokee Nation.

Elizabeth Watts, a young Cherokee girl, remembered the Civil War in the Cherokee Nation. She recalled that when her father entered the Union Army, she and her mother moved closer to a fort for protection. Despite this precaution, life was precarious. The family lost its meager belongings as bushwhackers and soldiers alike stripped the area. One day, four southern men came to the house and took any food they could find, including the green onions from the yard. Not content with theft, the group then turned to destruction, ripping open a feather bed and taking the tick for use in saddle blankets. When Elizabeth's mother attempted to hide her favorite dress by sitting on it, one man noticed and ripped the dress to shreds to show that the balance of power was entirely his. Similarly, when Rachel Lane's Cherokee grandparents told her of the Civil War, they shared a tale of devastation. When her grandfather returned from service in the army, he found everything gone and his wife dependent on the generosity of neighbors for mere survival.[1] Countless others recalled harrowing wartime experiences.

Residents of Indian Territory found the war to be an overwhelmingly ruinous event. The conflict had both immediate and long-term costs for American Indians. From 1861 to 1865, groups of Cherokees, Creeks, Choctaws, Chickasaws, and Seminoles supported both the Union and the Confederacy. They served as officers and enlisted men, suffered as civilians, and fled their nations as refugees. Their homeland endured great destruction both in the course of regular army operations and through the activities of bushwhackers and guerrillas. Having just begun recovering from the ordeal of removal, the nations faced an equally devastating upheaval in the Civil War.

The Cherokee Nation encapsulated much of the war experience in Indian Territory. As a large and important Native nation, this ethnic group could not escape this pivotal event in United States history. The Native American tribes held a unique position in nineteenth-century American society. As "domestic, dependent nations," as Supreme Court Justice John Marshall famously described them, American Indians maintained a position unlike any other minority group. Although much of their former political, economic, and numeric strength had declined, Cherokees retained a large measure of self-governance. They had their own form of government, as well as educational, judicial, and law enforcement systems. They entered the Civil War as a sovereign unit and maintained that status throughout the conflict. Led by an elected chief, the Cherokee Nation undertook diplomacy and foreign policy initiatives and managed domestic issues. Both the Confederate and the Federal governments had to negotiate with the Cherokees as peers if not equals. Native loyalty to either side could not be taken for granted, compelling North and South alike to earn the allegiance of the people of Indian Territory.

These Natives were not merely pawns or victims of white America's actions. Despite strong pressures from outside interests— local, state, and federal—and unfair and oppressive treatment meted out to them, American Indians often managed to maintain their sovereignty and retain considerable control over their own destiny. Historians may, in retrospect, point out diplomatic blunders and errors of judgment, but the more important point is that these choices, whether right or wrong, were made by the Indians.

The unique background of tribal members must be examined to understand the decisions made by them and their nation. The behavior of the members of the Cherokee Nation was more than just an immediate reaction to current circumstances. Centuries of existence as a distinct cultural group informed their choices and affected their experiences. Influences as varied as matrilineal descent, clan affiliations, economic distribution, and decentralized government combined to make the Native reaction to the Civil War distinct from that of other groups.

Tribal members also had varying levels of commitment to the idea of acculturation and conformity. The efforts of the federal government and religious organizations to push Natives into what they regarded as a more civilized way of living had achieved different degrees of success. Some tribal members had willingly embraced changes in religion, economy, politics, and lifestyle. This trend created a marked division among Cherokees regarding values and goals, as well as differing perceptions of the role of Native peoples in national events. Current leadership and internal factions therefore affected the Cherokee Nation's outlook.

Factions within the Cherokee Nation greatly influenced conduct during the war. Many Native decisions had far less to do with mainstream American events than with internal power struggles. As in other political units, support coalesced around groups with differing values and perspectives. Loyalty and rivalry played a role in countless individual decisions. Some of the discord grew out of the changing nature of Indian life, often reflected in the tension between "traditional" and "progressive" outlooks. Other strife stemmed from the recent struggles over removal. This catastrophic event had occurred only three decades prior to the Civil War, and its tremendous wounds had not healed. The Cherokees bore scars from the removal fight that would contribute to their division during the war. Cherokees, both families and individuals within the tribe, responded to the national crisis in ways influenced by a host of cultural and historical factors.

The Cherokee Nation became involved in the Civil War and endured a range of wartime tribulations. The indigenous example both mirrored and diverged from that of the rest of America. In many ways it closely approximated the experience of white southerners, who were more likely than their northern counterparts to suffer wartime shortages, enemy occupation, guerrilla raids, and forced relocation. Because of the shifting military control of Indian Territory, residents also experienced conditions similar to those of Unionists who lived amid a hostile majority in many sections of the Confederacy. Native people also endured the reality of the term "brothers' war," as did the populations of nearby states such as Missouri. The horrors of internecine conflict played out all too clearly in Indian Territory.

At the same time, their sovereign status, identity as a distinct cultural group, and position between the two main combatants combined to give the Cherokees a wartime experience unlike that of any other population. The nation operated as a distinct political and social unit throughout the war. Never members of either the Union or Confederacy in the same sense as the states, Indians had to protect their own interests while engaged in a larger struggle. The tribal government retained responsibility for its civilians, who faced numerous insecurities throughout the war. With delayed or inadequate financial support from the Confederacy and later the Union, the nation had to make provisions for relocating and feeding thousands of displaced residents. Participation of Indian men in the armies also differed from other groups. Confederate Indians fought in units raised directly from their nation and under terms outlined in treaties. They chose their own officers and retained a marked independence. Union Indian regiments had more white officers and less autonomy than did their southern brethren. Both groups existed as racial minorities, however, with all the prejudices of the day coming to bear on Indian soldiers, who were never accepted as equal to whites.

As historians strive to understand the Civil War, it is critical to include and interpret the experiences of all participants. The theater of the war encompassing the land of the Cherokees and other indigenous nations was never as important as the eastern theater, however. The location of national capitals, population density, and economic production combined to elevate the East to preeminence in both nineteenth-century and recent attention. The names Honey Springs, Ft. Gibson, and Chustenahlah will never become as familiar to Americans as Gettysburg, Antietam, or Chancellorsville. This observation need not demean or dismiss the importance of Indian Territory to an overall understanding of the Civil War. Neither Union nor Confederacy could afford to ignore this region during the war. Each spent money, supplies, and political capital in an attempt to control a border region rich in resources. The outcome of the war in the Cherokee Nation mattered to those engaged in the national crisis and it should matter to us as well.

The story of the Indian nations in the American Civil War is painful to read. Native people suffered in countless ways ranging from physical destruction to the dismantling of social systems.

Perhaps the greatest consequence of the war, however, was the loss of autonomy. Within four decades following the war's end, the Cherokees, along with the other four members of the Five Southeastern Nations, would cease to exist as political institutions recognized by the federal government. The conflict decimated their populations, shattered any fragile unity that may have translated into political clout, and brought the lands of Indian Territory to the attention of a wider group of Americans, both white and black. By the end of the century, railroad owners, cattle ranchers, exodusters (freedmen exiting the South), and many others flooded through and over the Indian nations, seeking new opportunities. The American Civil War marked the beginning of the end of the independent Five Nations.

*

This study is necessarily a combination of different historical approaches. It concentrates on a period of war and thus includes battles, troop movements and strategy; it is not a strictly military history of Indian Territory, however. There were few large battles in the Cherokee Nation and most military planners in Richmond and Washington probably knew little of the region's attributes. My focus is on the Cherokees and their choices, decisions, and experience—a history of a people in crisis.

The commitment of historians in recent decades to expand their focus beyond wealthy white males to include the roles of the poor, women, and racial minorities in history is clear in recent scholarship. Valuable contributions have been made in all fields by broadening historical study. In general, however, Civil War history lags behind this trend. Despite a tremendous outpouring of new studies of the war, inadequate attention has been paid to minority groups—thus the importance of this book. Few recent works have explored the role of American Indians in the war, and those that have are either quite broad or very narrowly focused.[2] Native Americans have never been central to the study or explanation of the Civil War. Yet Cherokees played an important role in the unfolding drama of the war; moreover, the war profoundly affected Cherokee life. It did not involve all Cherokee people equally, nor did all Cherokees influence the conduct of the war. Some individuals shaped the nation's participation in the war, especially members of the Cherokee elite.

John Ross was arguably the most important leader in the history of the Cherokee Nation. He was educated, wealthy, and powerful, and his views and actions defined the course of the nation in his many years as principal chief. Without doubt, he was a member of the Cherokee elite. A fine home, successful business, and undeniable political power testified to Ross's position in the nation. Of Scottish descent, speaking Cherokee as a second language, he shared few aspects of daily life with those he governed. However, the majority of Cherokee males continued to reelect Ross, choosing him as their leader in incredibly stressful times. The Cherokees had been convinced by removal that they must rely on their leaders to protect tribal autonomy.[3] The "great mass," as one Cherokee described them, of perhaps more traditional and less acculturated Cherokees recognized the importance of the elite.[4] These elites had achieved wealth and status, often by building on the advantages afforded them by non-Cherokee fathers, many of whom engaged in trade.

White ancestry was not requisite for power in the Cherokee Nation, however. John Ross's main rival after removal and through the 1860s was Stand Watie (Degatada). Only one-quarter white by blood, Watie did not learn English until adolescence. His full-blooded father had converted to Christianity, prompting him to drop his traditional name Oowatie in favor of the Euro-American styled David Watie. After the bloodshed surrounding the removal crisis, Stand Watie took a more active political role in the nation, serving as speaker on the Cherokee National Council while he ran businesses and practiced law. Thus, a commitment to capitalism, participation in the centralized national government, and a desire to shape the future of the nation were better indicators of elite status than simply blood quantum or wealth.

In the mid-nineteenth century the Cherokee Nation existed in a world dominated by non-Cherokee culture and institutions. The governments of the United States and later the Confederate States, comprised of presidents, congressmen, Indian agents, and military officers, wanted to deal with counterparts with similar skills. Reading and writing English, for example, remained a powerful tool of diplomacy, a tool possessed mainly by the elite.[5] Literate Cherokees left the bulk of historians' sources for the period in the form of newspapers, letters, political proceedings, and official records. One hundred forty-five years later we know the most about a minority of the Cherokee nation, but conversely, so did their contemporaries. The men and women in this book enjoyed power and prestige and notoriety beyond their numbers and played a critical role in the experience of the Cherokees in the American Civil War. It is to this group that we must look to find the motivations, rationales, and realities of the Cherokee experience. This is not to exclude other Cherokees who had little access to power. All Cherokees, indeed all residents of Indian Territory, were affected by the war. But to a great extent that experience—the entrance into and conduct of the war— was governed by the elite of the tribe.

It is important to note that while the elite of the Cherokees may have displayed hallmarks of acculturation—English literacy, capitalist enterprises, and Christian worship—they remained Cherokee, proudly so. Native Americans have always chosen certain characteristics of Euro-Americans to emulate. Since contact, cultural traits, economic strategies, and worldviews have been assessed and accepted or rejected by sovereign groups. Elite Cherokees incorporated elements of the dominant population's "civilization" while remaining Cherokee. John Ross, Stand Watie,

and other influential men wanted to preserve their Cherokee
identity. They believed in and fought for their ideas of the future
of the Cherokee Nation, not assimilation of the tribe into the
mainstream and loss of their Cherokee identity.

Terminology is often a tricky matter, especially when working
with a past so often defined by outsiders. The scholarly world
has come to no agreement on an acceptable way to refer to
those of Native and non-Native heritage. The term mixed-blood
has drawn some criticism from scholars in the field of Native
history, yet no suitable substitute has been offered. As historians
we strive to let our subjects speak for themselves, and the term
mixed-blood occurs frequently in nineteenth-century records. I
continue that usage here. Similarly, I occasionally use the terms
"progressive" and "traditional" as nineteenth-century observers
did, distinguishing between Indians who chose to move toward
assimilation and those who did not. There were distinctions in
the lifestyles of various Cherokees which reflected the influence
of Euro-American culture. Although these distinctions cannot
be wholly tied to parentage, there are connections between
"mixed-blood" heritage and "progressive" outlooks that cannot
be ignored. This is not to suggest that blood or genes determine
lifestyle, but instead that cultural exposure affects worldview. We
need to recognize that mixed race parentage represented different cultural norms, values, and beliefs, and to a lesser extent
that mixed race heritage could position people differently in
native society. We know that by the nineteenth century, Cherokees
had adopted a stronger sense of race that affected many elements
of life and would be relevant in the crisis of the 1860s.[6]

*

Change in Cherokee views and values came in part from their
long contact with Euro-Americans, dating to the explorations of
DeSoto in the mid-sixteenth century. The Cherokee tribe occupied
a region now included in Georgia, eastern Tennessee and western

North Carolina. Never the sole indigenous inhabitants of the region, the Cherokees and other members of the Five Tribes represented the most powerful native presence in the area by the nineteenth century. The southeastern tribes maintained decentralized authority, with primary loyalty given to local groupings until white contact forced a restructuring of government.[7] Southeastern people combined hunting and agriculture in nearly equal balance, and prior to contact with Europeans they had no domesticated livestock. Men provided dietary protein by hunting animals such as deer, bear, waterfowl, and wild turkey, and by fishing in lakes and rivers. Women raised corn, beans, and squash in fields they owned and gathered berries, nuts, and seeds. Females also prepared food, made clothing, and cared for children and the household. Men tended to politics, warfare, and much of the ceremonial life.[8] The gender division that governed daily life was quite clear. It afforded each gender a share of responsibility, and thus value for the continued success of the community. Far from being the drudges, or slaves, described by male European observers, Native women enjoyed respect and power from their status as life-givers, both literally as mothers and figuratively as agriculturalists. Women also gained status from the cultural practice of exogamous matrilineal descent, meaning that children traced their position in society through their mother's line and could not marry within her kin group. Men, especially the wealthy, practiced polygyny, often marrying sisters. Clan membership, inherited through the mothers, provided the most important tie an individual had to the community, and that relationship was also exogamous. The clan, rather than any tribal government, regulated intratribal relations, including punishment for murder and adultery.[9]

Native communities, operating as independent entities, reacted differently to the various pressures and changes introduced by Europeans. Although Native societies are sometimes regarded as slow to change, the Cherokees experienced major institutional restructuring in the nineteenth century.[10] They became involved in a capitalist/market economy through commercial hunting, livestock production, and agriculture. Cherokees forged ties to the southern business community, solidified by such developments as Masonic Order and Protestant church membership. Entrepreneurs took advantage of the new opportunities offered by a diversifying economy, opening taverns, ferries, and stores. Many wealthy Natives even adopted the South's system of coerced labor and became substantial owners of black slaves.[11] These changes separated some Indians from others, encouraging different goals and values. Traditional gender and kinship roles tended to break down as women yielded authority over agricultural production and children moved away from matrilineal descent.[12]

Economic diversification brought changes in political organization. A centralized form of government developed in the mid-eighteenth century, creating a new polity—the Cherokee Nation.[13] By the early nineteenth century, the Cherokee Nation had a legislature, written constitution, national treasury, court system, and a lighthorse (police force). To some extent this transformation was intended to silence critics who declared Native people "savages" without organized government and codified laws, but it also furthered the interests of those accumulating property and following the "white road."[14] Changes in government required corresponding modifications in leadership and society. As it matured, the political system moved the Cherokee people away from a kinship-based organization. Traditional measures of leadership—prowess in hunting and warfare, generosity, and courage—no longer met the needs of the nation. Dealings with whites required various skills held by assimilated men, such as an understanding of American culture and the English language. Mixed heritage often afforded men education, personal wealth, and business experience from a white father as well as a position in the tribe through their native mother's clan affiliations. Thus white contact instigated the rise of mixed-blood leaders such as Cherokee Chief John Ross and his counterparts among the other Five Tribes.[15] Economic prosperity often coincided with political power. Signers of the 1827 Cherokee Constitution owned farms four times the average size in the nation, and by using slave labor they produced a crop five to six times the average. The "common" or average members of the tribe, in contrast, struggled to survive as subsistence farmers, succeeding in good years, suffering in bad, and remaining suspicious of rapid changes.

Many powerful families became Protestants, and organized religion became another wedge dividing members of the Five Tribes. Protestant missionaries brought much more than religious zeal to the Indian country. They brought a firmly rooted belief in the efficacy of hard work, sobriety, individual accountability, and progress.[16] Thus they often became natural allies of mixed-bloods who pressed for acculturation within tribes.[17] Attempts to control the behavior of believers caused conflict within communities, however. For example, the leaders of one Cherokee town asked that the missionaries be removed because they had forbidden Christian Cherokees to attend council meetings, thereby weakening the bonds of community participation. When individuals followed Christianity and rejected their traditional beliefs, they embraced a distinct world view and value system.[18]

Initiated by missionaries, white influenced education also contributed to the breakdown of societal norms and oral tradition. Teachers, either white or white-educated, stressed mastery of English and conformity to white dress, manners, and values. This attitude had a perhaps intangible but nonetheless important effect on the community. Mixed ancestry children excelled in these schools while poorer children from traditional families did not.[19] Thus the tribally-funded educational system both catered to and reinforced the ascendancy of a tribal elite.[20] Government

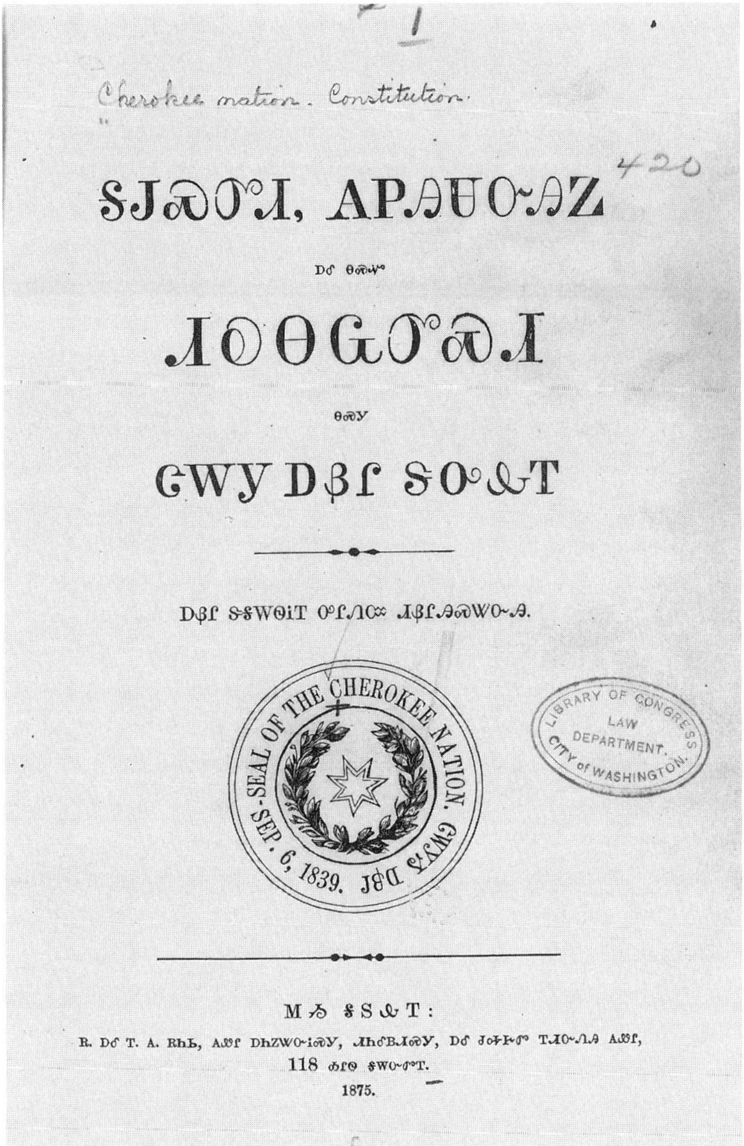

The Cherokee Nation's constitution was modeled on the U.S. Constitution, 1827. Courtesy of the Library of Congress.

agents generally reinforced this division, disparaging tradition and favoring "civilization." Superintendent Elias Rector expressed typical views: "[A] single year makes so little difference in the degree of civilization of the apathetic and indolent Indian."[21] This attitude determined that the focus of the government's time and resources would be toward acculturation, with little attention to the needs of traditionals.

The growing division between acculturated and traditional members of the Cherokees lay under the surface of daily life. Many traditionals seemed content to allow the more aggressive members to accumulate wealth, education, and embrace Christianity, so long as this trend did not greatly alter their own lifestyle. They generally entrusted the management of foreign relations to those whom they believed had the necessary English language skills and an understanding of white diplomacy.[22] By the 1820s, the Cherokee Nation elected two progressives as top executives and made rapid strides toward acculturation. To be sure, there were challenges to this movement toward Americanization. In 1827, a traditional leader named White Path called for a rejection of the new Cherokee constitution and other trappings of white society, including Christianity. His message attracted a large group of followers, most of whom had not previously participated in politics. The perceived threat to their way of life spurred them to action, but the resistance came too late. Tension simmered below the surface of Cherokee life, ready to emerge during their greatest crisis to date—removal.

CHAPTER 1

Prelude to War

The Cherokee Nation hereby cede relinquish and convey to the United States all the lands owned claimed or possessed by them east of the Mississippi River.

CHEROKEE TREATY OF 1835

The American Civil War began in 1861, but its roots lay much deeper in the country's past. The storm that broke upon Lincoln's election in November of 1860 had been brewing for decades. Legislation such as the Missouri Compromise attempted to patch over the growing differences between economies based on free and slave labor, though to little avail. Thomas Jefferson's "fire bell in the night" had at last begun to sound.[1] The bloodshed of the war had even been foreshadowed in the sectional violence that wracked "Bleeding Kansas" in the 1850s. The Civil War in Indian Territory followed a similar path; the outbreak of war followed decades of tension and transition. Residents of the Cherokee Nation had split over issues in the past and would do so again. The ongoing transformation which so tested the strength of the Indian nation resulted both from the Native society's own development and its forced interaction with Euro-American culture. Contacts with whites aggravated and prolonged internal divisions within Native communities. These divisions had a powerful influence on the reaction of the nation to the sectional crisis.

The removal policy of the United States government in the early nineteenth century was one of the greatest challenges to tribal unity and sovereignty faced by American Indians. The idea of moving Native people out of areas inhabited by whites certainly was not new in the nineteenth century. Thomas Jefferson had envisioned enclaves or reservations in the West to hold primitive people until they could achieve a sufficient level of civilization to be fit neighbors for industrious yeoman farmers. Indeed, the Southeastern Indian Nations had already signed numerous treaties yielding their eastern land to the expanding population of white southerners. What differed in the 1820s and 1830s was the virulence of the attacks against Indian sovereignty and land ownership. This intense offensive gained power from the attitude of the president of the United States. Andrew Jackson was indissolubly linked to Indian removal, and his election in 1828 sounded a death knell for Native sovereignty.

Jackson developed an unusual and somewhat ambiguous relationship with Native people. Although once a military ally of the Cherokee (he fought with them at the battle of Horseshoe Bend in 1814), President Jackson favored personal and political expediency over loyalty to former comrades by supporting southern interests determined to remove Native inhabitants.[2] Georgia initiated an aggressive campaign to rid itself of the Cherokees. Tactics included disavowing tribal sovereignty by extending state laws over Indian land and annexing the territory into the state. White southerners regarded the state's actions as a license to disregard Native landholding rights. They blatantly moved onto Cherokee land, seized improvements, and in general terrorized Native inhabitants. The Indian Removal Act of 1830 put the weight of the federal government behind state efforts. The Office of Indian Affairs, the federally mandated protector of Native rights, championed the cause of removal through its agents.

Removal sparked deep divisions within the Cherokee Nation. The split was bitter, long-lasting, and directly related to the division of the nation during the Civil War. The trauma of civil strife engendered by the removal crisis left fissures in the community that would open again in a few decades. As the federal government increased pressure on the nation, two distinct groups emerged. The majority of the tribe adamantly opposed removal, and Principal Chief John Ross and his followers pledged to uphold the will of the majority. Many of those opposed to relinquishing their homelands were traditionalists and probably hereditarily Cherokee; their political power, however, was vested in the elites holding tribal offices. This reflected the core of Native politics—rule by consensus. Ross would carry out the will of the citizens or lose power. A few leaders began to have second thoughts as pressures increased and Georgia perpetrated ever more outrageous crimes against the Cherokee people. This change in heart gained momentum from a younger generation of Cherokees. Educated in Connecticut, married to white women, and engaged in the pursuit of individual wealth, John Ridge and his cousin Elias Boudinot represented the rising generation of acculturated men whose skills and ambitions suited them to lead their people.[3]

The motivations of this group were both national and personal. As Georgia continued extralegal maneuvers unchecked by Jackson's government, any hope for an equitable settlement dwindled. The Cherokees appealed to the highest legal authority, the United States Supreme Court, and discovered that favorable rulings provided no practical protection. Under these trying circumstances, removal could be viewed as a positive step for the Cherokee people. In addition, removal would personally benefit members of the negotiating party. They would gain both political and economic power because the United States government rewarded those who sided with its interests.[4]

Striking out for their share of power, the Ridge faction decided to treat with the United States government for the sale of the Cherokee homeland. Two separate delegations arrived in Washington in 1834: John Ridge's to negotiate and John Ross's to fight. United States officials gladly dealt with Ridge and negotiated a treaty, even though Chief John Ross was the duly elected Principal Chief of the Cherokees. The Treaty of New Echota was signed by Major Ridge and Boudinot at a council meeting attended by about two percent of the Cherokee people.[5] A petition from 16,000 Cherokee citizens failed to sway the United States Senate against the fraudulent treaty, and ratification passed Congress by a single vote. In a tragic but not unusual example of United States Indian affairs, a fraction of the population had committed the majority to move. The Ridge faction headed west soon after removal became official, but the bulk of the nation did nothing as the two-year deadline approached. When the time arrived, the federal government sent in the military to force removal of the Cherokees to Indian Territory. The resulting tragedy was the infamous Trail of Tears.[6]

Although all Five Southeastern Nations endured removal, it was the Cherokees' removal journey, which they called "the trail where we cried," that captured American sympathy. Portrayed in novels and paintings, it was one of the most widely known events in American Indian history. Historian William T. Hagan referred to horrors of Nazi behavior in discussing the Indian removals of the nineteenth century.[7] Indeed, the Cherokees suffered tremendously during removal, experiencing at least a twenty-five percent loss in population and possibly an even higher rate.[8] The loss of loved ones and family structure was only one part of the suffering. The unwilling migrants left behind personal property only to arrive in a strange land with few possessions. The divisions and factions created by removal, however, were more important to the Cherokees' future than

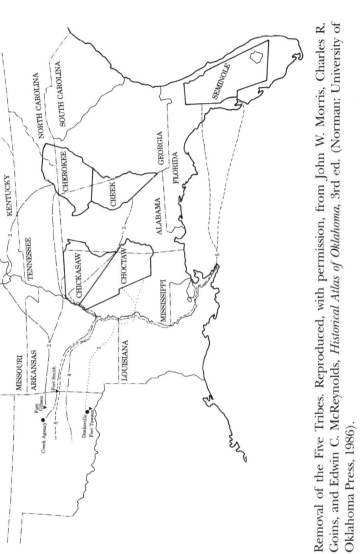

Removal of the Five Tribes. Reproduced, with permission, from John W. Morris, Charles R. Goins, and Edwin C. McReynolds, *Historical Atlas of Oklahoma*, 3rd ed. (Norman: University of Oklahoma Press, 1986).

the hardships of the move. Material losses were made up in one decade, but the hatred lasted for several.

Those who survived the trek arrived at Fort Gibson in north-eastern Indian Territory and began reconstructing their lives in the Cherokee Nation's new homeland.[9] Homes, churches, and businesses could be rebuilt, but unity could not. Relocation did not heal the wounds created by the dissent over removal. Tempers ran high, exacerbated by the horrors of the migration. On June 22, 1839, three treaty signers—Elias Boudinot, John Ridge, and his father, Major Ridge—were assassinated by Cherokees as punishment for violating the law forbidding the sale of tribal lands. Boudinot's brother, Stand Watie, quickly became the leader of the pro-treaty opposition to the Ross anti-removal faction. Thus, in the mid-1840s, the Cherokee Nation resembled an armed camp as retaliatory violence escalated. Officials recorded thirty-four murders within one year. With an official peace agreement reached in 1846, the issue of retribution died down, but the memories remained and would resurface in periods of stress. Other problems occupied the Cherokees—some directly from the new location, others from the existing divisions within the tribe.[10] A political power struggle arose between the Ross majority and the "Old Settlers" who had migrated west in the 1820s. The conflict and divisions over removal remained fresh and prevented harmonious settlement. From a low point in 1839, rife with murders and vengeful violence, the Cherokees slowly rebuilt their nation. The divisions endured, however, and would reemerge in the 1860s.

After a difficult period of adjustment, the Cherokees seemed to be settling into their new homes. Areas such as Tahlequah developed into permanent settlements. Government, religious, and civic institutions served the people. Peace and prosperity did not last, however. Forces at work both within and beyond the tribes portended another period of chaos and loss for the Cherokees. The issues that split the tribe in the 1830s remained. Personal jealousies and near blood feuds divided powerful leaders.

Some remnant of traditional kinship networks created an atmosphere in which relatives did not forgive, much less forget past wrongs. The Ridge-Watie and Ross families who had spilled blood in the recent past would have the opportunity to do so again under the banner of a military conflict.

Distrust of the federal government also remained an issue. Few could forget the hardship brought on by the U.S. removal policy. The same government planned for still more removals. Why should any Cherokee trust or aid that institution again? The Cherokee Nation did maintain a formal relationship with the federal government, but it was rarely concluded to the satisfaction of the Indians who continued to press for full compliance with treaty rights. The Cherokees who survived the upheavals of the 1830s and 1840s were headed directly into another life altering crisis in the 1860s.

SLAVERY

The nations of Indian Territory were fully aware of the sectional tensions that divided the North and South. Conflict that wracked Kansas in the late antebellum period spilled over into the neighboring Cherokee Nation. The election of 1860 reportedly caused "excitement and bitterness of feeling" throughout the region. The contentious issue of slavery, cause of the major controversy in the territories, also plagued Native peoples. Their long-term exposure to the political, economic, and social systems of white America ensured that the southeastern Indians would not be free of the impending sectional crisis.[11]

Southeastern Indians held African Americans in chattel slavery, which differed from earlier forms of captivity among indigenous cultures such as the holding of war prisoners. The degree of involvement varied both between and within nations, but the practice remained viable. Generations of contact with

Indian Territory cabin. Post-removal culture in Indian Territory resembled the rest of the South. Courtesy of Western History Collections, University of Oklahoma.

the southern plantation economy provided a model for this practice. The development of the slave system among Native people was intriguing and complex.[12] The ownership of humans contradicts a popular view of Native Americans as existing in egalitarian, subsistence level societies; however, slavery constituted part of a general acceptance of the dominant white society's economic, social, and political institutions. The process of assimilation encompassed both negative and positive aspects of the ascendant culture.

The Cherokee adoption of black slavery evolved as a direct result of an increased demand for labor accompanying the American government's encouragement of large scale agriculture among the Indians.[13] When Native peoples adopted the white culture's relationship to blacks, they also took on white racial prejudice. African Americans who moved into Indian Country prior to the adoption of slavery often found a warm reception from people who had no concept of race. As racial slavery became established in the Southeastern Nations, however, so too did the idea of separation of races based on skin tones.[14] While full-scale chattel slavery, which granted complete control to masters, developed gradually within Cherokee society, restrictive slave regulations appeared by the 1820s. Even so, the Cherokee slave codes prior to removal remained much less comprehensive than those in surrounding states.[15]

Slavery caused economic, political and social divisions within the Cherokee nation. The adoption of a slave system allowed for more rapid development of classes within the tribe. Contemporary Ethan Allen Hitchcock noted the existence of distinct economic divisions in society soon after the Cherokee relocation to Indian Territory.[16] Similar to the rest of the American South, Native slaveholding had the potential to concentrate great wealth in the hands of individuals. Owning African slaves became a form of capital accumulation which ran counter to more traditional concepts of tribalism.[17] Political disputes over the role of slavery in Indian society usually emerged as part of a larger debate over the speed of assimilation. Native populations had long participated in extensive trade networks involving commodities, but growing cash crops marked a change for southeastern tribes. Because slavery so clearly connected Indians to Euro-American patterns of production for a market economy, it could be viewed as a strong feature of acculturation that contributed to a loss of Native traditions. The connection between slavery and social position further divided Indian communities. Indian slaveholders tended to be both elite and of mixed heritage. A list of the largest slaveholders in the Cherokee Nation reveals the influence of important mixed-blood families such as Adair, Vann, Ross, and Murrell.[18] Slave owning represented a symbol of progress toward acculturation that furthered the divide in Cherokee society.[19]

By the 1850s, slavery in the Indian nations evolved into a system less harsh than that of most southern plantations but no longer approximating earlier relationships between blacks and Indians. The Cherokees passed restrictive legislation that denied non-Cherokee blacks the right to own property, read and write, or even remain in the Cherokee Nation once freed.[20] That the Cherokee slaves were not forbidden to carry weapons until 1841 testified to the less restrictive nature of the earlier system. By the Civil War period, however, Indian-owned slaves lost many of their former liberties. Some historians insist that at this point slavery among Indians was little different from that in the white South. But eyewitnesses had another impression. Union soldier Wiley Britton declared that slavery never existed in the Cherokee Nation in the same way as the rest of the South. He based his understanding on observations of black people who lived among the Cherokees. He noted that they never offered the deference and respect to Indians that characterized their behavior around white men. It was true, however, that Britton and his colleagues were members of the Union military force and may have represented both authority and an opportunity for freedom.[21]

The Indian nations soon became involved in the national debate over the future of the slave system. It is doubtful that the Indians would have joined this controversy without outside influence, as they had accepted slavery for over a century with little dissension. External pressures arrived, however, in the form of missionaries and government agents. Thus the national debate that divided churches and political parties into northern and southern factions received a thorough airing in the Indian nations.[22]

RELIGIOUS DIVISIONS

Missionaries had long been a part of Indian life, especially since the fervor of the Second Great Awakening inspired evangelicalism. They established a presence in the several nations prior to removal, operating churches and schools in an effort to bring Christianity to these particular nonbelievers. Operations did not cease during the upheaval of the 1830s. Many missionaries simply transferred their good intentions and resumed work in Indian Territory. The most dedicated practitioners aided the tribes in their fight to remain in their homeland. The Reverend Samuel Worcester offered an example of his devotion. In 1831 Georgia tried to divide the Cherokees from their white supporters by making it illegal for whites to enter Cherokee land without a state license. Viewing this as an abrogation of Cherokee sovereignty, several missionaries defied the new law and were arrested. Worcester (together with Elizur Butler) endured prison for over a year before he returned to the Cherokees. His challenge to state laws formed the basis of the Supreme Court case *Worcester v. Georgia*, which found Georgia's actions to be unconstitutional.

Worcester continued to preach, translate, and print the gospel for the Cherokee people until he died in Tahlequah in 1859.[23]

Missionaries in Indian Territory worked under the supervision of missionary societies, usually based in the North. These bodies, such as the American Board of Commissioners for Foreign Missions (ABCFM), passed judgment on doctrinal and spiritual matters. The missionaries had to manage all daily responsibilities of their churches, schools, and mission properties. Some administrators, however, kept a close watch on local issues such as mission labor and church membership. Indeed, at times the oversight committees seemed more interested in secular matters than those of the spiritual realm. They also injected into Indian Territory the growing political and moral dispute over slavery. The problem of excluding slaveholders from Christian services entangled the northern missionary boards in a difficult situation with regard to Indian converts.[24]

Missionaries in the Indian nations found themselves caught between the growing antislavery sentiments of their white officials and the political reality of powerful slaveholding Indians. Christian missions existed at the will of the tribes and could be removed by national decree as the Creeks had already done. Missions received funds, materials, and personnel from the boards, and thus could not operate without the support of both groups. Native leaders made it clear that they had not accepted the missions in order to be judged on the morality of slavery. The Cherokees had a law barring from their territory any teacher suspected of harboring abolitionist sentiments. On the other hand, antislavery sentiment in northern churches grew to the extent of demanding dismissal of slaveholding members from the congregation. This increasing tension eventually divided churches, and thus missionary boards, into northern and southern branches. The newly formed Methodist Episcopal Church South, for example, boasted 4,170 members in Indian Territory in 1861.[25]

A few strongly antislavery preachers, such as Evan and John Jones, had chosen to work in Indian Territory, but most missionaries seemed content to spread the gospel but avoid the complications of slavery. This did not imply ignorance of the issue; teachers and ministers were fully aware of the unsettling effect of the slavery debate among Indian communities. James Anderson Slover, a Southern Baptist Board schoolteacher, reported being questioned by the Indians about his views on slavery. He replied, to his questioners' satisfaction, that his work had nothing to do with slavery and that he would baptize slaveholders and slaves. Slover believed strongly that politics and religion were two different institutions, only one of which concerned him. John Edwards, a Princeton educated missionary, found slavery an "unbearable institution" but received masters and servants in communion and believed he could work among the Choctaws without giving offense. Other missionaries resisted the demands of northern boards to exclude slaveholders from church membership. Cherokee minister Thomas Wilkinson claimed that he could not practice religion according to his conscience under the antislavery Northern Baptists. Conscience aside, preaching abolitionism was not a practical approach in a slaveholding society. One missionary who strongly disapproved of slavery remarked that taking a stand against the practice would only have hindered "doing anything for these people in a Christian way and undo anything that had been done."[26]

Deeply felt differences over slavery began to divide the religious community. Slaveholders were often the wealthiest and most powerful families in a congregation. Ministers complying with board requirements to expel slaveholders might find themselves preaching to an impoverished, politically powerless congregation of traditionals and slaves. Any perceived abolitionist activity in Indian Territory drew intense animosity. Missionaries discovered that the Indians drew no distinction between personal beliefs that slavery was immoral and actions of overt abolitionism. Regional newspapers added to the strong feelings by blaming missionaries for recent abolitionist troubles. Ironically, missionaries used these attacks as evidence presented to their northern boards showing that they were not in favor of slavery.[27] Attacks might come from either side, however, and some missionaries felt compelled to issue a statement that they were not advocates or apologists for slavery. This was tempered by an insistence on their right to determine membership and to continue admitting pious slaveholders.[28]

The employment of slaves at missions continually sparked reaction on both sides. Antislavery church members naturally opposed the holding of slaves by men of the church. This was a thorny situation for missionaries under the rule of northern boards; often these individuals tried to point out the absolute necessity of hiring slave labor for mission work. Cyrus Kingsbury noted that Indian Territory received inadequate free labor from the boards and could only meet its needs with trusted slave labor. Conversely, the impression that missionaries would aid slaves under their employ in their attempt to gain freedom drew censure from slaveowners.[29]

Much missionary correspondence reveals bewilderment that the debate over slavery should even have disrupted their work. They sought to spread Christianity among nonbelievers, and most realized that there were sins other than slavery to address. Many tried vainly to lift themselves above the heated issue and continue their work. One missionary working in Indian Territory counseled that if preachers kept quiet, did appropriate work, and did not interfere in politics, they probably would not be hindered. He expressed frustration at the position in which missionaries found themselves. "With some of our northern friends we are *proslavery* so much so that they wish to have no fellowship with us. Here we are dangerous abolitionists who need close watching and whose places ought to be supplied with men of a

PRELUDE TO WAR   31

different character." Such "embarrassments and perplexities"
caused some mission boards to give up on Indians completely,
as the American Board of Commissioners for Foreign Missions did
when it closed the Cherokee enterprise upon Worcester's death in
1859, forcing missionaries to scramble to find new supporters for
their work. The work of the ministry was being overwhelmed by
pressing political debates.[30]

ABOLITIONISTS

The majority of missionaries did not harbor abolitionist sentiments, but there were notable exceptions. While some occasionally
allowed a slave to work for wages and even purchase freedom,
such limited action hardly threatened the entrenched institution.
A few members of the clergy in Indian Territory, however, actively
proclaimed the antislavery message along with the Christian
gospel. Evan Jones and his son John, Baptist preachers to the
Cherokees, became the most famous of this group. The Northern
Baptist board supported and encouraged the Jones's abolitionist
leanings. Evan Jones complied with the demand to remove slaveholders from church membership, an act denounced by Reverend
Worcester. His task was not as daunting as that facing Samuel
Worcester and other missionaries, however, because his Baptist
mission attracted mostly nonslaveholding Cherokees. The rather
presumptuous action of judging and condemning Christians
within their own nation had serious repercussions. Jones was
branded an abolitionist and thus a threat to the stability of the
Cherokee Nation. This sort of activism would not be tolerated
by those promoting slavery in the Indian nations. Southern supporters encouraged resistance to any interference with slavery.[31]
     Much of the conflict over antislavery viewpoints in Indian
Territory occurred between whites. While many Indians seemed

capable of coexisting with differing stances on slavery, whites brought the larger national tensions into Indian Territory. Missionaries who worked and lived in the communities clearly exerted considerable influence among the Indian people, but they were not alone. Whites not affiliated with religious institutions, such as traders and Indian agents, also promoted their views on various issues. Much has been made of the fact that most government appointees to Indian Territory came from the South and represented, even if unconsciously, the cultural values and social arrangements of the region. A pro-Southern influence certainly existed, but Indian leaders continued to operate as autonomous, sovereign politicians with their own agenda.

Northern missionaries who promoted abolitionism often encountered tenacious opponents in the Indian agents. The case of Evan Jones and Cherokee Agent George Butler illustrates this point. Butler apparently believed it was his personal duty to protect slavery in the Cherokee Nation. He connected Indian prosperity with slaveholding, considering the institution useful in promoting the "rapid advancement" of the Cherokees. Butler went so far as to recommend the ownership of a black couple for all "wild" Indians as a civilizing element. He regarded missionaries such as Jones to be interlopers who should be removed, an opinion supported by Native slaveholders angered by their dismissal from Baptist churches. Butler criticized Jones and even the venerable Samuel Worcester for not wholeheartedly supporting slavery. As fear of abolitionism grew in neighboring Arkansas, Missouri, and Kansas, pressure increased to the point that agent Robert Cowart (Butler's replacement) expelled John Jones from the Cherokee Nation in 1860.[32]

Much of the tension and pressure in the communities of Indian Territory is hard to document, but in the Cherokee Nation the growing division took a concrete form. Men of the nation joined two opposing organizations that followed sectional lines. Southern sympathizing Cherokees became active in the Knights of the Golden Circle, a group with a membership restricted to slaveholders. A variety of camps developed out of this group, attracting primarily mixed-blood Cherokees. The Knights coupled their general support of slavery with a clear purpose of defending the Cherokee Nation from the "ravages of abolitionists" or other disruptions. After the war broke out, some Knights identified themselves as the Southern Rights Party and formed an organized opposition to John Ross's leadership.[33] Stand Watie was an early member of the Knights organization and, due to his rivalry with Ross, an obvious choice as leader of the affiliated political group.

Although the goals of the Knights were clear, this was not true of their opponents, who coalesced into a group known as the Keetoowah Society.[34] This society had shadowy origins and intentions and left a nebulous record of its existence. Most historians agree with the contemporary assertion that missionary Evan Jones stimulated the organization of the Keetoowah Society, and that it began in the Baptist congregation at Pea Vine in the Going Snake District. Confederate officials also accepted this account of the founding. Historian William McLoughlin, who has written most extensively on the Keetoowah Society, described it as a "syncretic religious-political society limited in membership to full-bloods." The group successfully blended traditional beliefs with elements of Christianity into a whole that ardently supported the unique status of the Cherokees as a sovereign people.[35]

While the precise origin of the Keetoowah Society is unclear, there is no doubt that it opposed the pro-Southern, acculturated members of the nation and intended to dominate Cherokee government. In 1859 the Keetoowah Society asserted that the Cherokees were divided into two parts that could not agree, and that it was the less powerful group. Their increasing political sophistication and participation sought to remedy this situation. Ironically, the Southern rights factions felt similarly dominated, referring to their opponent's "foot upon our necks." They derisively referred to the Keetoowahs as "Pins" (taken from the symbol worn on the lapel), and the term entered into common usage. Thus the lines were drawn in the Cherokee Nation. As the Keetoowah Society observed, these lines reflected the national government with Northern and Southern parties. Beyond their well-documented association with the Cherokees, there is some evidence that the Knights and the Keetoowahs spread to other nations—particularly the Pins to the Creeks and the Knights to the Choctaw.[36]

In addition to internal residents such as missionaries and agents, whites in neighboring states exerted considerable pressure on the Native people of Indian Territory. Residents of western Arkansas had always regarded Indian Territory as within their sphere of influence, perhaps anticipating a time when the area would be opened for white settlement. Local politicians and members of the press carefully followed certain issues in the nations, and antislavery activity certainly attracted attention. These prying neighbors had no compunction about expressing their opinions on the proper alignment of the Indian nations. Newspapers discussed the probable behavior of the "savages" on the Arkansas border. John Ross replied to such editorials, stressing the sovereignty of Native governments. He wanted outsiders to understand that the nations had their own interests and goals and were not merely pawns of white politicians.[37]

If writing letters had been the extent of white pressure on the slavery issue, Indian Territory might have fared better. But the coercion also took a violent turn. Overzealous whites subjected residents of the territory to harassment and threats reinforced by prominently displayed weapons. John Jones feared being banished to Arkansas, referring in a personal letter to the lawless mobs and vigilante committees he knew existed. The Cherokees were fortunate that their distance from the Texas border did not subject them to the same harassment from "Red River men" who disrupted church meetings in the Choctaw Nation.[38]

Another source of pressure on the Indian nations came from intermarried whites. Marriages between Indian women and white men were not uncommon, and such unions provided a strong tie between Indian Territory and neighboring states. Men from the surrounding region brought their pro-Southern values, economics, and social ties into mixed families. Men such as George Murrell, who married two of John Ross's nieces in succession, lived in two worlds. Murrell had a fine home in Park Hill, Cherokee Nation, and also owned plantations in Mississippi. Hunter's Home, like Ross's Rose Cottage, was renowned for its opulence and imported furnishings. Murrell moved between white and Indian societies, as did others, and commingled the influences. Ties between societies were also forged through business activities, as many acculturated Indians bought and sold goods within the southern economic sphere. An important group within the Indian nations thus felt strong bonds to the South—"natural sympathies," in John Ross's words—that would affect their decisions in the impending sectional crisis.[39]

By the late 1850s the Cherokees moved some distance from their roots as a southeastern indigenous nation. The influence of whites accelerated change in their society. The issues dividing mainstream American society also divided the Cherokees. Differences over the future of slavery drove a wedge into Cherokee society as elsewhere. Deep scars engendered by removal continued to influence their decisions. The Cherokees unfortunately held a unique position as a semi-autonomous nation on the border of two powerful groups preparing to wage war. The future would not be peaceful.

THE CHEROKEE NATION

On the eve of the Civil War, the Cherokee Nation was a hospitable place for many. Residents remembered a thriving community

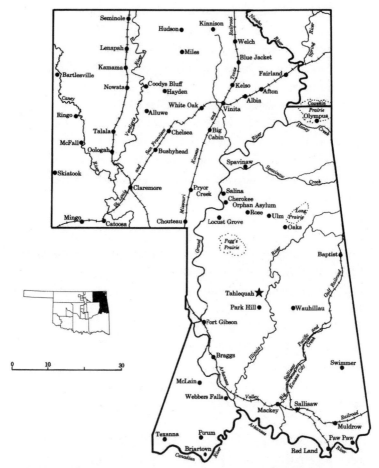

Cherokee Nation. Reproduced, with permission, from John W. Morris, Charles R. Goins, and Edwin C. McReynolds, *Historical Atlas of Oklahoma*, 3rd ed. (Norman: University of Oklahoma Press, 1986).

with plenty of food, clothing, churches and schools.[40] The nation encompassed the northeastern corner of Indian Territory, although the extreme tip had been carved out for the Seneca, Shawnee and Quapaw nations. The Cherokee Nation shared a border with Arkansas and Missouri to the east and the territory of Kansas to the north. The nation's shape resembled an inverted *L*, with the long leg stretching westward along the border with Kansas and the short side mirroring Arkansas. Neither southern Kansas nor western Arkansas was densely settled; border conflicts were not a major concern. The Creek Nation lay along the southern and western sides of Cherokee land and was also settled in the late 1830s.

This northeastern section of what is now Oklahoma bore more resemblance to the eastern homeland of the Five Nations than did the vast and arid western areas of the territory. The northeastern region enjoys average winter temperatures in the mid-30s, summer temperatures in the 80s, and average annual rainfall of over forty inches.[41] Located in the drainage basin of the Arkansas River, the Cherokee Nation had abundant surface water including several major rivers—the Verdigris, Grand, and Neosho. Forests extending west from the Arkansas border supported a diversity of plant and animal species, useful for hunting and gathering. Elsewhere, humid growing conditions, fertile soil, and a rolling landscape combined to create a habitat suitable for agriculture.

Agriculture supported most Cherokees and was even dubbed their "national employment" by a Cherokee Agent.[42] Many residents lived in log cabins typical of the period and practiced subsistence farming. Corn remained the staple crop, bolstered by wheat, oats, and cotton. Livestock, especially cattle, contributed to a diversified economy.[43] Women complemented the agricultural production with an impressive amount of spinning and weaving. Although most Cherokee families practiced subsistence farming, almost four thousand black slaves labored for Cherokee owners.[44] Other enterprises run by Cherokees included salt works and grain and lumber mills.

Many Cherokees settled in the southeastern section of their nation. Tahlequah was chosen as capital for its abundant spring water and proximity to forests for timber and prairies for hay.

It grew into a sizeable town with impressive brick buildings, such as the Cherokee Supreme Court. One could buy any number of items from several dry goods stores in town that accepted both cash and trade items such as beef, deer, raccoon and fox skins, wool, or beeswax.[45] An Arkansas newspaper described Tahlequah as "quiet and orderly, though rather dull, with four stores, three blacksmiths, a saddler, a shoemaker, a tailor and three taverns."[46] Nearby Park Hill became a relatively wealthy residential area, boasting the large homes of Chief John Ross, his brother Lewis, and their relative George Murrell. Murrell lived comfortably in a grand southern-style home attended by slaves. He also operated a dry goods store in Tahlequah. Murrell's affluent lifestyle was evident in an advertisement he placed to locate a runaway slave who wore a dress coat, silk hat, and blue frock coat with velvet collar.[47]

In addition to fashions, general American values also appeared in the Cherokee Nation. For example, Cherokees embraced the temperance movement, forming societies and sponsoring meetings. The temperance influence was strong enough for the Cherokee legislature to restrict alcohol in 1841, although the supply from outside the nation hardly faltered. Christian churches also influenced the temperance crusade and were well established in the nation by the 1850s. Missions under the auspices of the ABCFM, Methodists, and Baptists supported dozens of churches, schools, and missionaries, many of whom were Cherokee. Cherokees also joined other national groups such as the Freemasons, with the first Cherokee Nation Masonic Lodge opening in 1849.[48]

Cherokees valued other aspects of the Euro-American lifestyle. Mastery of English and other elements of white education became important skills for success by the mid-nineteenth century. Missionaries had long provided academies in the nation. The Cherokee government also supported public schools. The

Rose Cottage. John Ross lost his beautiful home to the ravages of war. Courtesy of Western History Collections, University of Oklahoma.

Park Hill Church and School. Religion and education were white influences altering Cherokee culture. Courtesy of Western History Collections, University of Oklahoma.

two seminaries opened in Tahlequah closed in 1856 due to lack of funds, however, and did not reopen until after the war. The government even paid to educate and care for orphans, a responsibility traditionally borne by kin and clan groups.[49]

Given the circumstances, the Cherokee people had made great strides after removal, but there was more to be done. Some residents lived in dire poverty. Cholera and other diseases threatened to sweep through areas with frightening consequences. Feuds lingering from the removal period occasionally erupted. Murders were not uncommon. Problems continued to plague the government, especially the chronic debt. Kansas politicians cast covetous eyes on Cherokee land, a perennial tension between whites and Cherokees.[50] By the late 1850s, of course, the debate over slavery cast a pall over the entire nation. That dispute would have a greater impact on Cherokees than they could have imagined.

CHAPTER 2

Decision for War

We do not wish our homes to become a battleground between the states and our soil to be rendered desolate and miserable by the horrors of civil war.

CHIEF JOHN ROSS

In 1861 the smell of war was in the air. No one could ignore the signs of tension in the country. Native nations could not escape the dispute between sections of the United States. Cherokees did not live in an isolated or static society. They held strong opinions on the topics of the day and in choosing sides were motivated by some of the same reasons as whites. People committed their allegiance based on loyalties to clan and family, views on slavery, belief in the obligations of treaty terms, and perceived opportunity for power and money. Above all, however, they made their choices as Cherokees, from a truly unique position of noncitizen residents of the United States. Their identity as Cherokees could never be separated from their actions, and most viewed choosing a side in the impending confrontation as imperative for both individual and tribal survival. The elite Cherokees, who by virtue of their political and economic power wielded a disproportionate influence in the nation, had to chart a course through the roiling waters of sectional controversy.

As the conflict approached, pressure from outside the territory increased. Politicians, neighbors, and ardent secessionists
scrambled to ensure that the Five Nations sided with the South
in the looming war. Their methods varied. Governor Henry Rector
of Arkansas tried to scare the Indians with vivid descriptions of
their certain ruin at the hands of the Yankees, while the citizens
of Boonsboro, Arkansas, bluntly demanded to know the intentions
of their Indian neighbors. Cherokee Chief John Ross answered
most correspondence diplomatically with soothing assertions of
the Cherokees' goodwill and desire for neutrality. His letters
reveal an impressive statesmanship and seemingly unending
patience with those determined to influence the Cherokee
Nation. "We do not wish our soil to become the battleground
between the states and our homes to be rendered desolate and
miserable by the horrors of civil war," he wrote to one Confederate
officer. In 1861, few could appreciate the exceptional accuracy
of Ross's prophetic words.[1]

OFFICIAL ALLIANCES

While whites from Arkansas and Texas applied pressure, Indian
leaders exercised their autonomy and began to make independent decisions which would lead their nations in different
directions. The Indian nations were already moving toward the
disunity that would prove to be a serious liability; a facade of unity
did not last through one intertribal council. The Chickasaws
called for a meeting on January 5, 1861, citing the need to renew
harmony and good feeling among the Five Nations. By the
time the council assembled in the Creek Nation in mid-February,
however, the Chickasaws did not even bother to send delegates.
William Ross, sent reluctantly by his uncle Chief John Ross, found
himself meeting only with Creeks and Seminoles. The council

John Ross, Principal Chief of the Cherokee Nation from 1828 to his death in 1866. Courtesy of the Oklahoma Historical Society.

accomplished little, and the absentee Chickasaws and Choctaws continued to pursue their own courses in regard to the war.[2]

The pressure placed on the Indian nations was intense and escalated as the outbreak of war drew near. Texans journeyed through Indian Territory, attending councils where they strongly stated the case for secession. Arkansas also sent emissaries to the chiefs. Indeed, Arkansas was so concerned over the allegiance of the Indian nations that its western counties hesitated to declare secession without them. Given so much state interest, it was unlikely that the new Confederate government would ignore the Indians. In March 1861, Richmond organized a Bureau of Indian Affairs and appointed David Hubbard as commissioner. Confederate intervention in the affairs of the Indian nations increased dramatically. Within a few months, three officials—Hubbard, Albert Pike, and Brigadier General Ben McCulloch—had missions to Indian Territory. Pike and McCulloch achieved the most, the former negotiating treaties of alliance and the latter recruiting military units.[3]

The response of the United States government aided Confederate efforts to secure the loyalty of the Indian nations. Some historians have accused the Lincoln administration of being idle in Indian affairs in 1861; on the contrary, it took steps that damaged the relationship with the tribes. For example, the Interior Department did nothing to rectify the deteriorating situation in the Office of Indian Affairs. The superintendent of the region openly supported an Indian alliance with the South, and agents under his supervision also expressed sympathies. The influence of white officials alone would not have been unduly harmful, but Confederate emissaries could point to alarming examples of current federal policy. Any diplomat willing to resort to scare tactics to win Indian alliance had ample ammunition. In a letter to Chief Ross, Confederate Commissioner Hubbard spelled out the impending evils of a Northern victory. Among the most serious threats was the loss of revenue.

Tribal trust funds were heavily invested in southern state bonds that would be forfeited in a war. In a poorly conceived decision, the U.S. government stopped the payment of tribal annuities in 1861, citing security concerns in transferring money to Indian Territory. While the goal of preventing funds from falling into enemy hands may have been understandable, the tribes suffered severely. The governments of the Five Nations relied heavily on these payments to fund their bureaucracy, including schools and police forces. The specter of bankruptcy was daunting.[4] Tribal leaders had little reason to trust a government that had suspended payments guaranteed by treaty.

The United States miscalculated the money issue and repeated the mistake in regard to defense. Unwilling to commit manpower to the task of retaining federal installations in early 1861, the army withdrew soldiers from the forts in Indian Territory. Colonel William H. Emory of the 1st United States Cavalry abandoned Forts Washita, Arbuckle, and Cobb in April 1861. Emory and the men from the garrisons fled the Chickasaw Nation to Kansas, led by a Delaware guide. Such a hasty retreat scarcely encouraged confidence in the United States military. The situation worsened as Texas troops quickly commandeered the forts, proving their readiness to cross into Indian land. Arkansas also announced that its troops were ready to guard the forts. The reaction of the Indians was understandable. Texans had a long history of violent Indian relations, and considering their recent proclivity for armed intervention, it made sense to be with them rather than against them.[5]

Inept United States actions and tensions within the nations created a situation in Indian Territory favorable to Confederate overtures. The Confederacy had chosen its emissaries well. Albert Pike, a colorful and wealthy Arkansas poet and lawyer, knew Indians better than many whites in the region. His reputation from obtaining a $140,000 settlement for the Creeks ensured at least a hearing by the tribes. Pike met with representatives of the

Five Nations and offered attractive terms for an alliance. The Confederacy understood the importance of securing its western border and was willing to promise money, political participation, and sovereignty in order to get it. Sovereignty included the right to determine citizenship, restrict residency within the nations, reject allotment and statehood, and control trade. The Confederacy also offered Indian delegates participation in its legislature, a privilege the United States had never conferred. Financial concerns were extremely important to the Indians, and they received protection of existing trust funds and guarantees of future annuity payments. The Confederate proposal incorporated many rights that the tribes had been unable to obtain from the federal government. If respected, such rights would have empowered the nations of Indian Territory. Four nations agreed to a Confederate alliance under these terms, leaving only the Cherokees outside the Confederate mantle.[6]

Resistance to a Confederate alliance did not necessarily reflect the will or opinions of the general population of the territory. Rather, it illuminated the divided power structure of the nations. Traditional members of each tribe, often described by witnesses as full-bloods, appeared opposed to breaking U.S. treaty obligations and entering a war; only in the Cherokee Nation did this group have access to power, however. The Keetoowah Society provided traditionals with organization and a vehicle for expression. Cherokee Chief Ross had always respected the will of the majority. By the 1860s, he had established a long history of defending majority rights against a vocal minority, now led by Stand Watie and loosely defined as the Treaty Party. An intense rivalry between these factions, stretching back over many years, clearly continued at the beginning of the Civil War.

The debate over removal had split the Cherokees violently, and the rift had barely healed. When John Ridge, his father Major Ridge, and cousin Elias Boudinot signed the Treaty of New Echota in 1835, they had become enemies of the state

Albert Pike served the Confederate government as both negotiator and military leader to the Cherokees. Courtesy of the Library of Congress.

represented by Chief John Ross. It was easy to use them to symbolize the blame for the tremendous hardships of the Trail of Tears. Their murder in 1839, probably at the hands of Ross supporters, almost destroyed the nation. The animosity engendered by the blame for removal and subsequent assassination festered in Cherokee society and politics. Despite a government brokered settlement between the groups in 1846, by 1861 Ross continued to face considerable hostility from "Treaty Party" adherents. The opposition coalesced around Stand Watie, brother of murdered Elias Boudinot. Stand Watie himself had escaped an assassination attempt, witnessed relatives and friends murdered, and killed a man he blamed for the death of his brother.[7] Watie was a strong leader and committed adversary. His group appeared ready to challenge and defy every position taken by the Ross government. Furthermore, the Treaty Party was already organized into an armed company, ready to defend themselves against any Ross party aggression. This influenced Ross's inclination to maintain neutrality and avoid entangling alliances with unproved governments. He spent much of the spring and summer of 1861 asserting the neutral position of his nation and waging an increasingly difficult battle to keep the Cherokee Nation unified.[8]

Albert Pike knew the Cherokees would be difficult to persuade. He respected the independence and intelligence of tribal leaders, but he equally understood tribal tensions and how to exploit them. Pike's correspondence with Secretary of State Robert Toombs explained the rivalries in the Cherokee Nation and declared his intention to deal with the "half-breeds" if Ross did not cooperate. The letter also shows an awareness that power was the bottom line of any negotiation; if the Confederacy could not prove its power to Ross there would be no treaty. As Pike remarked, the Cherokee chief was "very shrewd."[9]

Pike was camped in Park Hill, flying a flag emblazoned with a star for every Indian nation he had signed to allegiance with the Confederate States of America. He dearly wanted to add a star to represent the Cherokees, and he finally achieved it in August 1861. Chief Ross, after receiving approval from his executive council, called for a Cherokee national conference that month. The response drew about four thousand male participants. Ross's intentions were not immediately clear. He began with an

eloquent speech conveying his desire to ensure harmony, prosperity, and autonomy for Cherokees.[10]

> The great object with me has been to have the Cherokee
> people harmonious and united in the full and free exercise
> and enjoyment of all their rights of person and property.
> Union is strength; dissension is weakness, misery, ruin. In
> time of peace, enjoy peace together; in time of war, if
> war must come, fight together. As brothers live, as brothers
> die . . . . When your nationality ceases here, it will live
> nowhere else.[11]

The closing lines may have come as a surprise as Ross went on
to urge Cherokee citizens to give their consent for an alliance
with the Confederacy. They agreed without dissent. The Confederate treaty with the Cherokees, as well as the Senecas, Osages,
and Shawnees, was concluded in October 1861.

Ross's apparent change of attitude has long been a subject of
scrutiny. At first glance it appears to be a radical shift of position,
but closer examination shows Ross's decision to be consistent
with his long-standing goals. After leading an Indian nation for
several decades, Ross surely understood the inherent weaknesses
and problems associated with the nation's unique position as a
semi-autonomous state. His principal goal always had been to
preserve the existence of the Cherokee tribe with as much self-
government as possible. By the summer of 1861, the lack of
federal support, Confederate treaties negotiated with the mixed-
blood leaders of neighboring nations, and the increasing
involvement of the rival Watie faction with the Confederacy,
convinced Ross that a southern alliance made sense for the
Cherokee Nation. When the Cherokees signed their treaty on
October 7, 1861, all of the Five Nations were allies of the
Confederacy.[12] Ross worked to ensure harmony and unity
among the Five Nations. He even urged the pro-Union Creek

leader Opothleyahola to change his mind, as Ross had done, convinced it was the best course for the people they led. A civil war brewing among the Creeks would be the next diplomatic crisis Ross faced, however. More serious struggles and internal divisions lay in the future. Within a year the Cherokee Chief and over half of the citizens would ally with the Union. Ross's fear of divisions among his people would be realized.

The Confederacy had won the diplomatic race, at least in the short run. Confederate politicians, including President Jefferson Davis, had been wise enough to realize the importance of the Indian Nations in the overall scheme of an independent Confederacy. Much of the credit for this prescience accrued to efforts from bordering states. Texas and Arkansas had long been aware of and interested in the affairs of their Indian neighbors. They acted early to ensure a friendly border in case of war.

A lack of foresight on the part of the United States also aided the Confederate cause. Indian Territory agents and missionaries recognized the increased tension over slavery in the 1850s, yet the federal bureaucracy paid little attention. Both the Pierce and Buchanan administrations exhibited a pro-Southern tendency and thus had no interest in weakening the institution of slavery in Indian Territory. In addition to a lack of initiative in replacing southern agents, the Interior Department unwisely cut off desperately needed funds. The United States did nothing to reassure tribes of its support or continued protection, even after troops were withdrawn.[13] Given the situation, it was remarkable that any members of the Five Nations had sufficient confidence Washington to support the Union cause. The Five Nations acted as autonomous entities, choosing their own course based on their understanding of the situation. By not recognizing this, the Union proved to be its own worst enemy.

The official alliances were made, but for many Cherokees, as for many other Americans, choices and decisions about war were very personal. Ties to relatives outside the territory, the opinions of trusted friends such as missionaries, or personal animosities or friendships with leaders were strongly influential. Adherence to either the Treaty or Ross parties made the choice clear, but those less attuned to political rivalries were less certain of the proper course. Some argued that Cherokees cared little about the war until forced to make a decision.[14] The prospect of impending violence often pushed allegiances one way or the other. Ella Coody Robinson's family lived in a fourteen-room home with furnishings from New York. When raiders they identified as Kansas Jayhawkers entered the Cherokee Nation, the men of the family took action to defend themselves. Ella's stepfather and seventeen-year-old brother joined Watie's regiment, leaving the women at home under the protection of the white overseer.[15]

WAR COMES TO INDIAN TERRITORY

The struggle for the trans-Mississippi West included Indian Territory, and the region endured warfare from the winter of 1861 to the spring of 1865. Both North and South claimed the region over three and a half years of conflict that saw northern areas of the Cherokee and Creek Nations change hands repeatedly; neither side proved able to maintain absolute control of the Five Indian Nations. Nearly 18,000 Indian soldiers served in the ever-shifting contest, fighting for both the Union and Confederacy and occasionally switching sides. Cherokee men fought in a region known for brutality and intense partisanship. They fought as minorities struggling to retain autonomy in the face of racism and intense suffering. Despite a severe lack of training, supplies, and leadership, the Cherokees on both sides served their armies for the full course of the war, and even claimed to have the distinction of the last Confederate general to surrender.[16]

The Federal government did not make a strong start in Indian Territory and continued to lose ground from a lack of planning. With no government representatives in the Indian nations, the U.S. Army made no attempt to enlist Indians. While Union leadership debated whether Indians would make acceptable soldiers, the Confederate War Department moved quickly to organize in Indian Territory. Texan Ben McCulloch, with three regiments under his command, took charge of the military district embracing the Indian country. By mid-May 1861, Leroy Pope Walker, Confederate Secretary of War, had begun the process of accepting Indian troops. The first Indian regiment came from the Choctaw and Chickasaw nations, organized under the command of their agent Douglas Cooper. In a pattern that would be repeated with Cherokees, the Confederacy used the promise of readily available weapons to induce enlistment but failed to follow through.[17] From the beginning, officials knew that the availability of weapons bolstered Native commitment to the Confederate cause. Albert Pike told the secretary of state that to collect the Indians and "keep them long without arms would disgust them, and they would scatter over the country like partridges and never be got together again." He suggested that the weapons provided be "plain muzzle-loading rifle[s], large bore, with molds for conical bullets hollowed at the truncated end, . . . since revolvers cannot be had, and an Indian would not pick up a musket if it lay in the road."[18] Unfortunately, such requests often went unfulfilled as four years of warfare stretched the Confederacy thin. Other, more positive patterns emerged as additional Indian nations pledged troops to the Confederacy. Native leaders asserted their self-governance by boldly claiming the right to possess federal installations, even if it meant challenging the Texans, and retained the right to choose their own officers, a privilege rarely accorded minority units.[19]

When it came to the enlistment of Cherokees for Confederate service, the legacy of removal complicated the issue. The rival leaders of the Cherokee factions, John Ross and Stand Watie, understood the implications of military service. An armed body sanctioned by the Confederate States could be an important asset in the continuing power struggle within the Cherokee Nation. Those who enlisted with the Confederacy expected to gain power and prestige as well as the guns, rations, and uniforms unavailable to those who remained loyal to the distant Union government. As de facto political leader of the pro-removal Treaty party, Watie moved first. His supporters were eager to form a military force and received encouragement from whites. Those living east of the Cherokees recognized that a defended buffer to a possible Union attack from the west would beneficial. Arkansas residents urged Watie to train his followers "for the defense of the nation," thus protecting Arkansas's border. Arkansas citizens would even provide the guns.[20] For their part, Watie's followers believed it was imperative for their leader to take advantage of the new power source. William Adair and James Bell spoke of breaking free from the power of the dominant party and Ross's "tyranny."[21] The Confederate arrival had the potential to change the balance of power in the intratribal struggle. Watie's followers did not want to lose the advantage.

Ben McCulloch, the Texan given command of Indian Territory for the Confederacy, also realized the value of Cherokee manpower and gladly accepted Watie's assistance in the summer of 1861.[22] McCulloch seemed genuinely pleased by Cherokee participation but remained aware that he faced an unusual situation. Receiving Watie's men into the Confederate military was a political maneuver as well as a military decision. John Ross remained the elected Principal Chief of the Cherokee Nation, which had yet to sign a treaty of alliance with the Confederacy. McCulloch risked unraveling the diplomatic process by drawing troops from the officially neutral Cherokee Nation. Only Albert Pike was authorized to negotiate treaties with Indian Nations, but Confederate diplomacy lagged behind military reality. McCulloch broached the subject of Cherokee soldiers in correspondence with Ross in June 1861. Perhaps underestimating both the diplomacy and integrity of Chief Ross, McCulloch demanded that Cherokees be allowed to arm for the purpose of defense. Ross "respectfully declined," making it clear in his eloquent reply that he would not be pressured by the Confederate military. He feared two outcomes from the existence of an armed unit—loss of neutrality , which he regarded as the Cherokees' only hope of surviving the war, and the instigation of domestic strife and internal difficulties in the nation. The memory of armed camps of Cherokees in the 1840s was not easily forgotten.[23]

Chief Ross held a difficult position in mid-1861. His party could not participate in military exercises for fear of violating the tenuous neutrality it had carved out, nor did it wish to be unarmed in the face of Watie's organization. McCulloch granted Stand Watie a commission as colonel on July 12, 1861. Soon three hundred men mustered into Confederate service under Watie. McCulloch stationed this Cherokee force outside the nation's borders in the Cherokee Neutral Lands (present day Kansas) in deference to Ross's declared neutrality. Nevertheless, some Cherokees traveled even farther away to fight with the Confederacy in Missouri. Battlefield reports mentioned the presence of Cherokees at the bloody battle of Wilson's Creek on August 10, 1861. The battle was a baptism by fire with a twenty-three percent casualty rate, including Union General Nathanial Lyons. Meanwhile, Ross's party remained aware of the political advantages of forming a military unit, and Ross secured arms for his men as soon as circumstances allowed. On August 24, three days after the nation voted to join the Confederacy, the Cherokee Executive Committee hastened to inform McCulloch of the organization of a mounted regiment for Confederate service. McCulloch obviously would not turn away the offer of a regiment. He favored Watie's unit, however, and expanded it to a regimental size. In urging the Confederate War Department to attach Watie's men to his command, McCulloch

Stand Watie was a political and military leader of the Confederate Cherokees. Courtesy of Western History Collections, University of Oklahoma.

described the Cherokees as "half-breeds, who are educated men, and good soldiers anywhere, in or out of the Nation" but called Ross's followers "full-bloods."[24]

John Ross had appointed his nephew-by-marriage, John Drew, to raise the new military unit.[25] The political implications

of Drew's appointment were clear. If there had to be armed
Cherokees in Indian Territory, Ross intended to keep them
under his control. The Ross family loyalty had a long reach, and
although Drew was independent and respected by many, his
personal connection to the powerful chief remained strong.
Ross had always governed with the aid of his relatives, and the
new regiment merely extended this practice. The officers' roll
for Drew's regiment represented a list of important men in the
Cherokee Nation in the 1860s, including the chief's nephew
William Ross as lieutenant colonel and his brother-in-law as
adjutant.[26] Watie's force was similarly organized, including his
brother-in-law and sons. In many ways such organization reflected
tribal traditions. Kinship ties had been the strongest link binding
Native peoples, and Cherokees had always confronted danger
with their relatives beside them.

The creation of a unit of Ross supporters increased the rivalry
with Watie's party. Treaty party members expressed their outrage
that Ross had tried to undercut their power. Watie's brother-in-
law, James Bell, regarded the formation of Drew's regiment as a
threat to his faction's existence and warned Watie of the possibility of Ross's domination.[27] The first power struggle developed
over the naming of the Cherokee units. The right to be called
1st Cherokee Mounted Rifles was contested, even though Watie
had taken the field and received a colonel's commission more
than a month before Drew's unit even organized. Drew offered
the Confederacy a full regiment while Watie had been operating at battalion strength, which was a smaller force. The Treaty
Party rallied to increase Watie's group to regimental size, but it
still followed as the second regiment filled. Because both units
claimed the right to be called the First Cherokee Mounted Rifles,
common reference to either Drew's or Watie's unit became the
most practical designation.[28]

On the political front, the Treaty Party also provided the only
official Cherokee representative to the Confederate government:

Watie's nephew, Elias C. Boudinot. The treaties between the Confederate States of America and the various Indian nations provided for a tribal voice in the new national government. Only the Choctaws and the Cherokees managed to elect and send delegates to Richmond to fill seats in the Confederate Congress. There they offered insight into the conditions of their nations, primarily in the form of dissatisfaction with the Confederacy's support of Indian nations. Boudinot served as the Cherokee delegate for the duration of the war. He also served as the Indian delegate to the Committee on Indian Affairs when that position was created in 1864.[29]

By the fall of 1861, then, the sides were drawn and the players chosen. Indian men were now enlisted in opposing military forces whose goals potentially conflicted with Native interests. The previous year had been critical in determining the nature of the factions. The split within the Indian nations would continue until the bitter end, with serious repercussions for the future of Indian sovereignty.

The first military activity in Indian Territory involved Indian against Indian and had serious ramifications for the Indian-Confederate alliance. The southern Indian forces existed, in theory, to defend their nations. The general understanding was that the threat would come from Union forces, or perhaps from guerrillas or raiders lurking on the borders. Few expected the conflict to begin among their own people. The resultant spilling of Indian blood by Indian hands left a legacy of bitterness that rivaled the removal split of the 1830s.

In the fall of 1861, Cherokee troops would be embroiled in fighting fellow Indians in running battles that seemed to have little to do with their reasons for enlisting. They found themselves facing an "enemy" who was quite familiar—Creek Indians. Although the Creek Nation, like the Cherokee Nation, had officially allied with the Confederacy, it was far from united in that position. The treaty negotiations included only pro-Southern

Creek leaders and some opposition leaders found their forged signatures attached to the document binding their nation to a commitment they opposed.[30] Dissatisfied individuals and families rallied around Opothleyahola, an elderly Upper Creek spokesman who refused to abide by the treaty signed in July 1861.[31]

In 1861, Southern sympathizers empowered by Confederate promises of support dominated the Creek Nation. Pro-Union Creeks—or loyal Creeks, as they referred to themselves—felt increasingly threatened and gathered for mutual protection.[32] Opothleyahola no longer trusted Cherokee Chief John Ross, a former Indian ally in the fight against removal. He counted on the support of the Cherokees under Ross, believing Ross would hold true to his initial refusal to sign with the Confederacy. The news that Ross had altered his course and declared for the South was a major blow. Opposition leaders at first did not believe the report. Ross attempted to persuade the Creeks to join him in a Confederate alliance, and Lower Creek Chief Moty Kennard asked Ross to intervene in the hopes of alleviating the growing tension. Kennard and Ross feared an internal conflict, and these fears would soon be realized.[33]

The dreaded civil conflict occurred in November 1861 when Confederate forces under the command of Douglas Cooper converged on Opothleyahola's group, referred to as hostiles. Opothleyahola had anticipated this action and moved his people north toward the perceived safety of Union lines. In a series of three engagements—Round Mountain, Chusto-Talasah, and Chustenahlah—Confederate Indian forces aided by Texans drove several thousand pro-Union Cherokees, Creeks and Seminoles into a desperate trek to Kansas. Although these engagements were short and swift skirmishes, they had a profound impact on the course of the war for the Indians.

Cooper instigated the attacks on the loyal Indians, and later took full credit for the aggression in his report to Confederate Secretary of War Judah P. Benjamin. Cooper claimed knowledge of correspondence between Creek chiefs and the Federal government. He then misrepresented the connection to be an alliance, justifying his military action against civilians. The presence of a respected Native leader who opposed the Confederate cause annoyed Cooper.[34] Indeed, there is no evidence that Opothleyahola posed a serious military threat; he merely represented an alternative to a Confederate alliance for Indian Territory residents. Entire families flocked to his leadership and protection—hardly an offensive force. Regardless, Cooper pledged to "either compel submission . . . or drive him and his party from the field."[35]

Douglas Cooper commanded the 1st Choctaw and Chickasaw Mounted Rifles, the 1st Creek Regiment, the Creek and Seminole Battalion, and a detachment of Texas troops. He gained strength from the 9th Texas Cavalry when it marched through Indian Territory en route to Arkansas in November 1861. When the Texans paused at Boggy Depot they learned of Cooper's request for additional forces, and the officers detached five hundred men under Lt. Col. William Quayle for service in Indian Territory.[36]

The 1,400 white and Indian soldiers pursued Opothleyahola's group of families. Proceeding up the Deep Fork of the Canadian River, the Confederates found the loyal Indians' camp deserted and helped themselves to abandoned cattle and corn. It took Cooper four days to catch up to the civilian Creek entourage. Afterward he relied on captured prisoners for information. On November 19, 1861, the Confederates believed they had overtaken Opothleyahola's party when they saw smoke from fires, indicating a camp. The Confederates charged the supposed encampment only to find it recently vacated. The Texans under Quayle, eager for their first military encounter, impetuously rushed forward following a few scouts. The scouts led the cavalry directly into an ambush by concealed Creek and Seminole warriors. The result was chaos. Cooper formed the Choctaw and Chickasaw regiment for an attack, but the Texans were so far ahead that no one could fire safely. The officers hesitated and called out to ascertain the location of their troops. Darkness hampered the efforts of both sides, and intentionally set prairie fires only added to the confusion. The skirmish ended after a mere fifteen minutes, and casualties were correspondingly light.[37] The loyal Indians had disengaged in order to follow their fleeing families. The group headed northeast, forded the Arkansas River in the dark, and entered the Cherokee Nation.

The effect of the contest was evident the next day. The brief encounter had forced the loyal Creeks and Seminoles to flee in haste, leaving much of their wealth behind. Cooper's men rode into the abandoned camp and tallied their booty: Opothleyahola's buggy, twelve wagons, flour, sugar, coffee, salt, cattle, and ponies. Captured supplies were a welcome bonus for Confederate forces on the march, but their loss represented a serious blow to their owners. Because Opothleyahola's people were civilians, no government supported the group, and no army commissary supplied them. They subsisted on what they could carry and forage. Cooper's forces denied them all means of subsistence by taking their supplies and forcing them to run. The men of Opothleyahola's band had to wage delaying actions to allow the women and children time to move again. Unlike the majority of Civil War battles, the Confederates in Indian Territory were attacking a primarily civilian group. These were Indian men protecting their kin groups in a traditional manner, not an offensive army.[38]

The pursuit of the loyal Indians continued into December 1861, with weather and attrition adding to the hardship on both sides. Cooper caught up with the travelers in the Cherokee Nation. This development proved alarming because many Cherokees were known to be lukewarm Confederates, and the presence of dissidents might spark a defection. Rumors of an impending attack by Opothleyahola magnified the sense of urgency, although it is unlikely that this band of fleeing families intended to deliver an offensive blow against mounted soldiers. Cooper believed the information, elicited from a prisoner, and added Colonel John Drew's Cherokees to the Confederate effort. Drew commanded mostly full-blood men who had enlisted to defend their nation and were loyal to John Ross rather than to Jefferson Davis. The Confederacy had done little to encourage their devotion. The unit lacked flour, coffee, sugar, salt, and adequate clothes and blankets. The 1st Cherokee Mounted Rifles did not embrace the Confederate cause with the same dedication as their southern allies and probably were considered to be only a supporting force to the main thrust. Unfortunately for Cooper, Drew's men made first contact with Opothleyahola's people at Bird Creek. Ross' Cherokees remained eager to settle the Creek matter by diplomacy instead of conflict. With Cooper's approval, Major Thomas Pegg of Drew's regiment attempted to meet with Opothleyahola. The situation quickly degenerated into confusion. Pegg returned from his diplomatic mission empty-handed, and his report of Creeks painted for war alarmed Cooper. It also served to complete the disintegration of Drew's command. Men "slipped away" from camp and from Confederate military service that required them to fight friends and relatives. Some went home, others to Fort Gibson, and many joined the loyal Indians they were meant to fight.[39]

The defection of Drew's men should not have come as a surprise. The soldiers had enlisted out of loyalty to their chief and a belief in his assertion that the borders of their beloved nation must be protected. Drew's regiment was raised to combat enemies of the Cherokee Nation, not foes of the Confederacy. The Creeks posed no immediate threat to the Cherokees and thus did not fall under a strict definition of enemy. Many Cherokees had personal relationships with Creeks as neighbors in Indian Territory for over two decades. Furthermore, their chief had often expressed his desire to talk to Opothleyahola and other Creek leaders, not to shoot them. Ross even tried to

John Drew, nephew of Chief Ross, led Cherokee forces in the Confederate army until most of those in his command defected to the Union. Courtesy of the Oklahoma Historical Society.

keep Drew out of the confrontation by insisting that he was needed in his "own country." James McDaniel was among the men Cooper believed had gone over to the Union side. Chief Ross actually had sent McDaniel to contact Opothleyahola and to escort the Creek chief to Drew's headquarters or to Lewis Ross's house for a discussion of his grievances. It would have been an act of deception for McDaniel to fire on the fleeing Creeks. Hundreds of Cherokee soldiers also chose not to fight the "hostile" Creeks and Seminoles. Members of the Keetoowah Society in Drew's regiment could not fight fellow Keetoowahs in the loyal camp.[40] Without fanfare, they crossed over to Opothleyahola's group. Drew's men deserted the Confederate side rapidly, leaving behind tents, horses, and guns. Teamsters freighted supplies out of the empty camp while a chagrined Colonel Drew rode to Cooper's headquarters to report the debacle. Drew explained that his men's behavior was due to a "misconception of the character of the conflict between the Creeks, and from an indisposition to engage in strife with their immediate neighbors."[41] In other words, Cherokees knew an intertribal fight when they saw one and wanted no part of it. Cooper sent the Texans to evaluate the situation, and Drew resolutely pledged his remaining twenty-eight men for service.[42]

The battle of Chusto-Talasah, or Caving Banks (north of present-day Tulsa), went on despite the defection of the 1st Cherokee Mounted Rifles. The site was well-chosen for defense. Opothleyahola sheltered his warriors along the high banks (thirty feet in places) of Bird Creek. Cooper's men found it difficult to attack the natural stronghold, but they kept up the effort throughout the afternoon of December 9, 1861. After four hours of fighting, the loyal Creeks withdrew at dusk, and the Confederates regrouped in camp. That night they experienced the hardships of winter campaigning when three inches of snow fell. Cooper exaggerated enemy losses and claimed a victory at Chusto-Talasah—despite the fact that the dissident Creeks and Seminoles remained at large.[43]

After two engagements, Cooper was not confident in his ability to drive Opothleyahola from Confederate soil. The renegade band of families had proven itself difficult to overcome, and it appeared that more Cherokees were joining them. Cooper requested that white troops be stationed in the Cherokee Nation for their "moral effect," yet he was surprised when Colonel James McIntosh arrived with two thousand troops in the form of the 2nd Arkansas Mounted Rifles. The surprise resulted from McIntosh's bold assertion of command and immediate movement into the field. Cooper had planned on spending December at Fort Gibson rather than in an arduous winter campaign on the prairie. He did not join McIntosh in the ensuing battle. Instead, he was content to chase a few civilians around the northern part of the territory and grumbled that much more would have been accomplished if McIntosh had waited for him.[44]

McIntosh's pursuit of the loyal Creeks resulted in the battle of Chustenahlah on December 26, 1861. After four days in the field, he cut free from his baggage train. His men became aware of the enemy as they moved across the country. Opothleyahola also was aware of his pursuers and prepared to meet them yet again. The Creek leader always chose his ground carefully, with an eye to natural protection. A site along Shoal Creek met his requirements. The women, children, and supplies remained sheltered while warriors took up a fine defensive position half a mile to the south. Although McIntosh charged an enemy ensconced in a defensive position, his assault succeeded. The Confederates dislodged the Creeks and Seminoles with a rapid onslaught. Many defenders fought fiercely, but the majority were routed and fled to the north. McIntosh's men continued the chase, cutting down pro-Union Indians wherever they scattered.[45]

The battle of Chustenahlah doomed the unfortunate loyal Indians. Colonel McIntosh reported that the enemy was completely broken up and its forces scattered. The military defeat of the warriors, represented by retreat from the field, was less critical than the material losses the civilians sustained. The Confederates pushed north to the Creek encampment, "shooting and cutting down the enemy" along the way, and wreaked havoc there. They captured 180 people and property including wagons, horses, cattle, and sheep. The losses deprived the Creeks and

Seminoles of the means to continue their journey. Both food and transportation were severely reduced, and the women and children who escaped were forced to flee on foot. Stand Watie's 2nd Cherokee Mounted Rifles arrived after the battle and inflicted further misfortune by seizing nearly a thousand head of livestock and hundreds of ponies. Colonel Cooper's men also chased the dislocated Creeks and Seminoles toward the Kansas border until forced back due to the bitter winter weather.[46] The first military campaign in Indian Territory had ended.[47]

THE WIDER WAR

The western theater of the Civil War has rarely received its due attention. Both at the time and for over a century after the war, Americans gave greater importance to the armies, commanders, and battles of the East.[48] This focus relegated the western and trans-Mississippi theaters, and their Indian combatants, to a minor role in the history of the war. The trans-Mississippi West may not have been the most critical strategic area for Lincoln and Davis and their military advisors, but it did play an important role in the struggle for control of Confederate Territory. The importance to the Cherokees loomed even larger than to the national audiences. Their new homeland—all the land they would likely ever control—was here, and two powerful nations now fought over it.

The war had come home to the Cherokees in the summer of 1861. When the two national armies clashed at Wilson's Creek near Springfield Missouri, they were less than one hundred miles from the Cherokee Nation. Although reports on the subject conflicted, it appeared that some Cherokees, led by Joel Mayes, fought with the Confederacy. Perhaps, as some assert, they fired the volley that killed Union General Nathaniel Lyons.[49] Despite the death of a notable general, the Union continued to advance

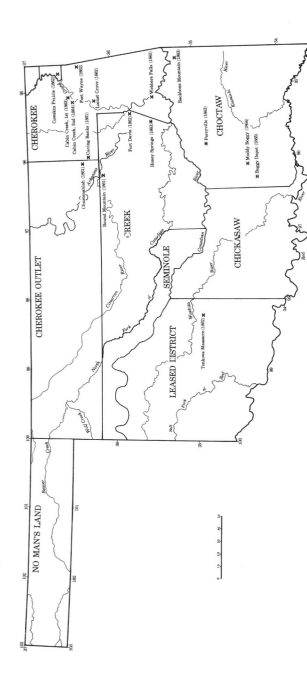

Civil War Battle Sites. Reproduced, with permission, from John W. Morris, Charles R. Goins, and Edwin C. McReynolds, *Historical Atlas of Oklahoma*, 3rd ed. (Norman: University of Oklahoma Press, 1986).

its cause in the West. By the spring of 1862, the Union had demonstrated its dominance in the trans-Mississippi West, effectively pushing the Confederates out of Missouri and hoping to continue that thrust into Arkansas.

Union General Samuel Curtis commanded over ten thousand men in the Army of the West. This was an army of men from western states, with ranks heavily filled by German immigrants. Confederate Major General Earl Van Dorn attempted to counter the strong Union push into Arkansas in early March 1862. He led the 16,000-strong Confederate Army of the West and hoped to secure the region for an eventual offensive into Missouri. As Curtis deployed in Benton County, Arkansas, Van Dorn had to meet him and so gathered up all available Confederate forces. The call for troops went out to Albert Pike, now in command of the Confederate forces in Indian Territory as a result of his work in negotiating the Indian treaties. He responded to orders from McCulloch and marched his men to Arkansas to participate in the battle of Pea Ridge, March 7–8, 1862, despite treaty assurances that Indian forces would not leave their nations without their chiefs' consent.[50]

In the haste to concentrate men against the Union invasion, no one consulted with the tribes about fighting outside their territory; such a consultation was required by the 1861 treaties. A march to Bentonville, Arkansas, clearly did not involve a direct threat to Indian homes or families. This was not a matter of self-defense. Furthermore, Confederate Indian regiments had good reason to be disgruntled with military administration. They had not been paid. Families relied on military wages, and soldiers were determined to get what was due them. The Choctaw and Chickasaw regiment saw no reason to serve without compensation and refused to march. Pike paid out the funds he had on hand for other purposes in an effort to induce loyalty to the cause, but bemoaned the delay of several days. Even after the payment, however, the Choctaws and Chickasaws lacked enthusiasm, following slowly on the march. Drew's Cherokees also moved out reluctantly even as they were cheered on by Chief Ross, who asserted his faith in their loyalty. Few Indians could muster enthusiasm for the trek across the border into Arkansas, and only Watie's regiment moved with alacrity.[51]

The Indian soldiers were marching toward an unknown experience. They were the greenest of green troops due to their unfamiliarity with conventional military training. Native enlistees showed little tolerance for military drill or discipline and rarely received any. Scant attention had been paid to their preparation for duty, neither in outfitting nor training. They had spent little time in practicing battlefield maneuvers, and generally disdained infantry service, preferring instead to be mounted on horseback. Even worse, the troops had not trained in the use of artillery, an oversight that would soon haunt the Confederacy.

Pea Ridge would be a major battle in the competition for dominance in the West. Twenty-six thousand troops fought over two days in a struggle that resulted in nearly six thousand casualties. On the cold evening of March 7, with snow blanketing the hills, Van Dorn's men completed an exhausting march around the Union rear. With their otherwise superior numbers weakened through exhaustion and a lack of ammunition, the Confederates attacked on the Union left flank, north of Leestown. Curtis moved to counter the uncoordinated assaults, and the day passed in heavy fighting. Soldiers on the Confederate right fled after the deaths of both General McCulloch and his second-in-command General McIntosh; both men were killed within fifteen minutes of each other. On March 8, Curtis then counterattacked and forced Van Dorn to withdraw from the field in defeat.[52]

The battle of Pea Ridge was not a success for the thousand Indian troops or the Confederacy. The lagging Choctaw, Chickasaw and Creek units missed the battle altogether. Pike and the Cherokee regiments caught up with the Confederate force late on March 6. The following day exhausted troops were ordered to advance on the Leestown section of the battlefield as part of McCulloch's attack. Texas units led the charge on the Confederate right wing, followed by Stand Watie's dismounted men, and finally John Drew's mounted Cherokees. The Indian troops immediately came up against a Union battery and cavalry force, which they quickly captured in an exciting charge. After this initial success, however, the situation grew chaotic. The captured, unspiked Union cannons were useless because the Indians had never been trained in the use of artillery.[53] The thrill of the charge soon changed to panic when Colonel Peter Osterhaus directed Union guns to lob shells toward the unseasoned Indian troops. Terrified by the heavy fire, the Cherokees sought shelter in the woods and lost the advantage. The confusion worsened as the Indian troops remained pinned down by heavy fire and Generals McCulloch and McIntosh were killed. By late afternoon, Pike assumed command of units near him and determined to withdraw from the field and seek out Van Dorn.

The general disintegration of the Confederate line unsettled the already disorganized Indian troops, most of whom fled the field. This was not the type of fighting that the Cherokee soldiers had expected and many simply threw down their arms and went home.[54] Drew's men headed back to Indian Territory and their nation, which they had been reluctant to leave in the first place. After traveling forty miles, Pike finally rejoined his men in the Cherokee Nation.[55] Watie's unit took a position on the extreme right of the Confederate line and later stayed to guard the supply train during the rapid retreat, but this was little consolation for an otherwise disastrous day. The sweep for prisoners after the Confederate defeat netted at least eleven Indians, all of whom were shot as they tried to escape during a transfer to Springfield.[56] The Pea Ridge affair ended ingloriously for both the Confederacy and its Indian allies.[57] It was another in a string of defeats for the Confederacy in the West.

Attention remained on eastern events as the war's second year progressed. The battle of Pea Ridge was soon eclipsed by the sensational news of the USS *Monitor* versus the CSS *Virginia* engagement that dominates discussions of March 1862 even to the present day. Although few outside the nation noticed, the first year of the war had been confusing for the Cherokees. The conflict already had tested and broken bonds of kinship and loyalty, but the worst division was yet to come.

CHAPTER 3

War in the Territory

I beg your men to bury all old animosities and remember only that all are now fighting for the honour, independence and safety of the Confederate States and the Cherokee people.

ALBERT PIKE

The spring of 1862 found the Confederate Indians scattered and disorganized. Major General Van Dorn lost interest in the Indian forces after Pea Ridge, perhaps even before. His report on the battle praised every white commander he could recall but never once mentioned the Native troops on the battlefield. Letters from observers to Richmond described Van Dorn as "having nothing to do with" the Indian forces.[1] He essentially cut them loose from Confederate operations, offering only a vague mandate to annoy the enemy in Indian country. Colonel Drew's men returned to the Cherokee Nation after having left some sick and wounded soldiers at the Dwight Mission near Salisaw. A Cherokee schoolgirl in Van Buren, Arkansas, witnessed the return of troops and described them as "a terrible looking crowd, bringing their wounded with them." Their arrival disturbed the routine of the town as schools, churches, and stores were filled with the wounded.[2] With his remaining men, Pike ventured far into the heart of Indian Territory rather than patrolling its borders. Only Watie's regiment remained on the edges of Indian country, occasionally encountering small groups of the enemy.[3] If the Federals were to invade they would move in from the north or east, but the Confederate Indian troops remained in the south-central region, apparently to avoid confrontation.[4]

The concentration of forces in the Choctaw Nation worried the Cherokee chief whose country was in the path of the most likely line of invasion. Ross's correspondence with Confederate officials in 1862 revealed his concerns. He urged Pike to pay attention to the unprotected borders of Indian Territory and asked that troops be sent to protect the region around the Cherokee capital. Arguing for the importance of safeguarding the national treasury and papers, Ross achieved a significant political goal in having Drew's men posted in the nation. This regiment, raised under Ross's direct order and commanded by a relative, was posted in the area around Park Hill and Tahlequah, fulfilling several objectives. Ross provided military protection to the homes and businesses of his followers, thus strengthening their allegiance to him. He also ensured that pro-Ross men were armed and authorized to be in a region already harassed by anti-Ross forces under Watie. Perhaps most importantly, Ross had his regiment with him should Union troops arrive in the Cherokee Nation. In this way the clever politician was prepared to resist by force any Union encroachment and also able to use his assembled military strength as a bargaining tool with the Federals.[5]

FEDERAL INVASION OF INDIAN TERRITORY

Ross was wise to be prepared because Federal forces were indeed on the way to Indian Territory. A longstanding rumor, the oft-discussed Union advance became a reality in the spring of 1862. Confederate Indians had skirmished with the enemy previously, but the offensive launched in 1862 marked the beginning of a concerted Federal effort to regain the area. The foray into Confederate territory was the culmination of a long process in which thousands of Indians had enlisted in the Union army. The Federal government accepted the idea of Indian troops very slowly. From the Iroquois to the Creeks, American Indians were not welcome in the United States Army in 1862.[6]

Enlistment of Indians was not a simple process. Forming and sending a Union force into Indian Territory took a long time. Commissioner William P. Dole, upon learning of the organization of Indian troops into the Confederate military service, urged the Secretary of the Interior to convince the United States War Department to enlist loyal Indians. The army finally began enrolling Indian soldiers for a planned invasion into Indian Territory in February 1862. The eager Indian enlistees were understandably upset when progress ceased. Frustrated chiefs subsequently held their own council and stated their intent to undertake the expedition themselves. Tribal leaders retained responsibility for the well-being of their people despite the ravages of disease, poverty, and displacement, and they meant to achieve it by any means necessary. Only news of Confederate military activity in northern Indian Territory dissuaded them from their independent course.

The plan to invade Indian Territory using refugee troops did not die completely, but obstacles remained. The army's second call for Indian enlistment in April 1862 initially provoked suspicion among the refugees because of the failure of the first attempt. The arrival of two thousand guns, as well as the later distribution of spoils from war, added credibility to the second effort. Native leaders had long gained adherents based on their ability to follow through on promises, so tangible evidence of the Union's commitment to military action helped to convince Indian men to trust the army recruiters. The enlistment effort suffered a further setback when General Samuel D. Sturgis,

commanding the Department of Kansas, issued an order pro-
hibiting enrollment of Indians and threatening arrest for those
who continued such enlistment. This order was not enforced,
however, and enrollment soon filled two Indian regiments under
the command of General James Blunt. The refugee soldiers
apparently enlisted in the hope that the Union Army would
return them to their homes.[7] More than any ideological debate,
or even loyalty to leaders or factions, the quest to return to their
homeland, an essential component in Native lives, drove these
men to action. Nevertheless, pro-Union refugees stranded in
Kansas had to endure a long delay before joining the Northern
Army. By the middle of 1862, the Federal Army finally boasted two
regiments of Indians, and in the summer they put them to use.[8]

James Blunt now had command of the Department of Kansas,
which included Indian Territory. He planned to regain control
of the Cherokee Nation by sending white units from Kansas,
Wisconsin, Indiana, and Ohio along with the two Indian regiments. The First Indian Home Guard (IHG) consisted of Creeks
and Seminoles, while Cherokees, Choctaws, Chickasaws, and
Osages joined Creeks in the Second IHG. These men were
ready to serve the Federal government wearing ill-fitting blue
uniforms and carrying antiquated "Indian rifles," but their own
interests provided a greater motivation than any sense of duty.
When they marched south they carried with them the hopes of
thousands of Cherokees, Creeks, and Seminoles who desperately
wanted to return home. Many family members from the Kansas
refugee camps followed in the wake of the military columns,
expecting the invasion would establish Federal control over
Indian Territory and allow them to return to a normal life.
Fathers, sons, and brothers painted their faces, sang war songs,
and set off on the long anticipated journey.

The different goals of the army and the Office of Indian
Affairs (OIA), however, foretold problems for the conquest of
Indian Territory. As the commanding officer put it, one could

be "ground between the millstones of the Indian and war departments."[9] Eager to regain control of the area, especially to protect Kansas and Missouri from raiding activities, the army was willing to use Indian troops, but the expedition generated scant northern interest. The Indian soldiers, on the other hand, had a greater desire to return home rather than win glory for the military. Refugee leaders were aware of the gap between the objectives of their warriors and those of the army, and they worked to see that their plans were given priority. With Blunt at headquarters, the Indian troops would be under the command of Colonel William Weer, a Kansas Jayhawker with a fondness for the bottle and little empathy for troops who were not white. He complained of the constant questioning of his intentions on the expedition. He took no interest in inquiries he found "puzzling" and did little to ease the anxiety of his Native troops. He noted that the "Indians seemed to be filled with a dread of white men," but only *after* mentioning that he had to "come down heavy" in order to "overcome the thousand excuses" of the Indians.[10]

Weer did not understand the distrust of white involvement in Indian affairs, however well-founded it may have been. The army had no plan to repatriate the refugee soldiers. Days before the beginning of the march, Weer asked his superiors what he should do with the Indians once they reached their country. He later complained about "want of instructions as to the Indians." The invasion was clearly more complicated than the government had anticipated. Loyal Cherokees inquired about the future status of the property of those who had seceded. The Union enlisted Cherokees would be entering their country as an occupying force and retribution would surely follow. White officers recognized the likelihood of "jayhawking" and demanded revolvers before they marched.[11]

The invasion force included 1,600 recently enlisted Indian troops as well as white cavalry, infantry, and batteries, raising the total strength to about six thousand men. The target was the

Cherokee Nation; the Confederate Cherokee force was led by Stand Watie. After leaving Baxter Springs, Kansas, and heading down the Neosho River, the column crossed into Cherokee territory on June 28, 1862, an event that failed to gain much attention in a nation focused on the fall of New Orleans and the behavior of Benjamin "Beast" Butler. Indeed, the Union occupation of New Orleans would last far longer than that of the Cherokee Nation; Weer's men remained for only twenty days.

Because resistance melted away as Watie withdrew southward, Weer continued to march his troops farther into hostile territory without a clear objective or tangible results. The main body of the invasion force commanded by Colonel Frederick Salomon headed down the west side of the Grand River to Cabin Creek. Weer took a detachment of men along the east side of the river in an effort to engage enemy forces. Colonel Jewell's Sixth Kansas Cavalry spent a day chasing the elusive Stand Watie then moved on to Locust Grove, where Weer's men startled the Confederate camp of Colonel J. J. Clarkson.[12] The element of surprise worked in the Union's favor as the Confederates were unable to organize and eventually surrendered 110 men. The victory here boosted the morale of the pro-Union Indians. Some of Clarkson's men escaped to Tahlequah, where tales of their defeat encouraged Cherokee enlistment in the victorious Union army. Perhaps even more impressive than the news of success was the distribution of the spoils of the fight: some sixty wagons of ammunition and salt, sixty-four mule teams, and large quantities of other provisions. Here, at last, was an army in which men could believe. It is worth noting, however, that the Indian troops could have any spoils *except* army supplies. Gunpowder was given to Indian officers, but enlisted men made due with a large quantity of civilian clothing found in the captured wagons.

The success at Locust Grove was one of the invasion's high points. The expedition soon made camp twelve miles north of

Fort Gibson. It was hot, Weer was often drunk, and his white troops became restless. The situation deteriorated when supplies failed to arrive, yet Weer took no action. On July 18, Colonel Salomon cited the lack of contact with headquarters, dwindling rations, and a loss of confidence in the commander as cause to arrest Colonel Weer and take control of the expedition. Upon assuming command, Salomon immediately ordered the withdrawal of white forces from Indian country. The Indian regiments were to remain behind to maintain a Union presence.[13]

The abandonment of Indian Territory was a major blow to pro-Union Indians, but the short-lived expedition produced notable results. The Union gained important manpower through its invasion of the Cherokee Nation. With Pike's Confederate forces concentrated in the southeastern region, only Drew and Watie had troops available to combat the invasion, and Drew's men seemed an unlikely choice to hold off a Union thrust after their defection at Chusto-Talasah. Many Cherokees clearly felt a primary loyalty to Chief Ross and did not care to risk their lives for the Confederate cause. By early July more than six hundred of Drew's men defected to the Union.[14] Weer reported 1,500 new recruits from Cherokee country who filled the undermanned Second Indian Home Guard and the newly created third regiment under the command of Colonel William A. Phillips, a former reporter for the *New York Tribune*.

More important to the Union cause than the rank-and-file Cherokees who joined the army, however, was the most important political figure in Indian Territory—Cherokee Chief John Ross. Federal forces had arrived in the Cherokee capital of Tahlequah at a time when Ross made no secret of his unhappiness with Confederate military efforts. By 1862, he did not believe that the Confederacy had done all it could for its Cherokee allies. Letters to officials cited a list of concerns, including the "destitute condition of the Cherokee troops and of their families," the need for better defense of the region, the control of "white men roaming through the Indian country," and a better commander for Indian troops.[15] When no one addressed these conditions, Ross looked to the other side for redress.

Union officials had prepared to take advantage of Ross's wavering commitment to the Confederacy. Missionary Evan Jones accompanied the Union force and carried a letter to Ross from Superintendent of Indian Affairs William Coffin. The letter was meant to assure Ross of the United States's belated interest in treaty obligations. Although Weer asserted that "Ross is undoubtedly with us, and will come out openly when we reach there," the chief switched teams diffidently. An ally of the Confederacy, Ross initially refused to grant Weer an interview. Ross's pledge to the Confederacy had been made in good faith and was not lightly broken. His ultimate loyalty, however, was to the Cherokee people, who now seemed better served by the strengthening Union forces on their doorstep. Weer solved the uncomfortable situation by ordering Captain Harris Greeno to arrest and immediately parole the Chief and several relatives and supporters at Rose Cottage, Ross's Park Hill home, on July 15, 1862.[16] This timely measure forestalled a desperate call from the Confederacy for Cherokee male conscription—which Cooper had demanded Ross to issue—as well as orders for Drew's officers to report for duty to repel the enemy invasion. Such instructions were embarrassing to men who prided themselves on their integrity but had given up on the Confederate cause. Captain Greeno attempted to encourage the pro-Union sentiments he believed Drew's men harbored, addressing them at length and recalling the recent victories of Federal forces at Shiloh, Pea Ridge, and New Orleans.[17] Many men then followed him back to the Union camp and joined the Third Indian Home Guard. When Greeno marched out of Park Hill, escorting John Ross and his family to Union territory, most of the Ross faction allied itself with the Union for the remainder of the war. The Cherokee Nation was officially divided.[18]

The Cherokees now faced more turmoil than ever. The withdrawal of Weer's expedition left only Indian troops in the territory. The Native remnants of the Federal invasion force quickly realized their vulnerability, and their officers consolidated them into a brigade. This morale-boosting action was not enough to forestall the disillusionment that swept the Indian soldiers. They had staked their hope for the future on this invasion and were now sorely disappointed. Such dissatisfaction led to a wave of desertions. The OIA agents appointed to accompany the expedition reported a widespread belief that the army had abandoned the Indian people to a cruel fate. They predicted that soldiers' families would be "ruthlessly murdered," as would all who had expressed joy at the arrival of Union forces.[19]

Fear of violence and intimidation radiated throughout the Cherokee Nation for both pro-Union and pro-Confederate Indians and the few remaining whites in the region. Union officers found Chief Ross concerned about the safety of the family and followers who remained in Indian Territory. Captain Greeno reported that the "loyal people" in the area were very badly frightened because there were "bushwhackers in every direction."[20] Recent murders and robberies in the area alarmed everyone. In expressing the situation to Abraham Lincoln, Ross said the Cherokee people were left "in a position fraught with distress, danger and ruin." Stand Watie's forces received the blame for the depredations. Men who defected from the First Cherokee Regiment had ample reason to expect retaliation from former comrades still in the Confederate service. The existing factional feud grew worse following the desertion of Drew's men, whom Watie's followers viewed as traitors. Earlier in the spring, General Watie's nephew had killed and scalped Chunestootie, one of Drew's men. Such activities did not, in the words of the general, "tend to reconcile the factions already too bitter for the good of the country," although he claimed the victim had been hostile to "southern people and their institutions."[21]

The Cherokee, Creek, and Seminole families who had trailed the Union invasion into Indian country also feared for their lives. This fear came not only from the threat of direct violence, but also from their inability to reoccupy homes or plant crops because of marauding troops and bushwhackers. Anarchy reigned as neither side was powerful enough to restore order. All witnesses in Indian Territory testified to the destruction and ruin that plagued the region. The men who were supposed to free their homes from the grip of war watched as "wholesale ruin, open pillage and plunder" became the norm. Chief Ross's own family lost homes and belongings amid indiscriminate violence. It seemed that everyone bore the ravages of the war.[22]

Although many Cherokees suffered from the instability of war, their chief fared comparably better. After his capture by Union forces, Ross left the nation along with his wife and sister-in-law, carrying as well as their personal belongings the Cherokee government's papers from Rose Cottage. Many Cherokees who fled the civil unrest remained close to the nation, just over the border in Union-held Kansas. But John Ross, the principal chief of the Cherokee Nation, could do little good for his people and their cause if he remained in exile and cut off from the channels of power. With the encouragement of Union general James Blunt, then, Ross soon headed east to his wife's family home. In 1844 the chief had married Mary Brian Stapler, an affluent Quaker girl from Wilmington, Delaware.[23] The eastern connection now served him well, as his family could live in safety and comfort in her house in Philadelphia while he represented the Cherokees in Washington, D.C.

Ross had a difficult task. The Lincoln administration had little energy to focus on the affairs of Indian nations in the summer of 1862. Ross arrived to plead his case as the Peninsula Campaign fizzled and the problem of what to do with McClellan loomed large. Furthermore, as Ross was the head of a nation still officially allied with the Confederacy, he had to prove his loyalty to the United States before asking for government support. He obtained the endorsement of General Blunt who wrote to Secretary of War Edwin M. Stanton on Ross's behalf. Blunt declared a large majority of Cherokees to be loyal and clearly grasped their difficult situation. He explained that the Cherokee Confederate alliance was prompted by self-preservation due to the lack of Federal government contact, and that once the Union forces showed up the Cherokees joined their side.[24]

As the leader of an autonomous nation, Ross did not expect censure from the president of the United States. Ross blamed the Cherokees' defection to the South on the Union's failure to protect them in 1861, and in the same breath insisted that Lincoln's administration now live up to its treaty obligations to provide protection. President Lincoln took some time to warm to this idea, referring to the "multitude of cares claiming my constant attention" and his inability to confirm facts which might excuse the Cherokee Nation for "making a treaty with a portion of the people of the United States in open rebellion against the government thereof." The president did pledge to prevent the overrun of Cherokee country by the enemy, a promise that Ross needed.[25] For his part, John Ross remained firmly in the Union camp for the duration of the conflict. Four of his sons served in the Union army, and one died while being held as a prisoner.[26]

As the summer of 1862 wound to a close, the Union faced disappointments on every front. Union General John Pope's short-lived command ended with the loss at Second Bull Run, and the Mississippi River remained out of Union control. In Indian Territory, the Union's failure to prove its dominance in the summer of 1862 increased agitation to reestablish Federal control in the region. The Confederates fared little better in the Territory and military officers on both sides waged political warfare for the remainder of the year as conditions in the area deteriorated. The fallout found Albert Pike, the only Confederate officer who attempted to respect the Confederate Indian treaties, pushed out of the army with his position taken by Douglass Cooper.[27] General T. C. Hindman now commanded the Confederacy's Trans-Mississippi District and would soon turn his aggressive style toward western Arkansas and Indian Territory. Union Colonel William Phillips, a former Kansas free soil advocate, earned command of the reorganized Indian Brigade in early 1863. Phillips's leadership was a positive step for the Indian Home Guards, whom he would lead back to their lands in 1863. More significant than his subsequent military actions, however, Phillips appeared sensitive to the enormous suffering of civilians. His correspondence reflected an understanding of how injurious a proclamation of Union allegiance could be without the manpower to support it. He urged his superiors against encouraging displays of Union loyalty before the Union military could realistically support any followers.[28]

   The ebb and flow of interest in and troops committed to Indian Territory wreaked havoc with the lives of its citizens. In the fall of 1862, Confederates under Cooper remained outside the Cherokee Nation, south of the Arkansas River. On the southern side of the Arkansas, at the confluence with the Grand River, Confederates built Fort Davis directly across from Fort Gibson. Although Cooper had two to three thousand men and a new stronghold, he reportedly considered retreating even farther south to the Canadian River. This left the Union with a tenuous jurisdiction over the Cherokee Nation, but it could really only claim control of the region west of the Grand River. When Salomon retreated to Baxter Springs he left behind the Indian Home Guard troops. Colonel Robert Furnas consolidated these forces with the First Kansas battery to form a brigade. Such a small force could do little to alter the situation in the Cherokee Nation. Minor raids occurred—two to three hundred men to Fort Gibson, three to four hundred men to Tahlequah—but little stability resulted from the weak thrusts. Once Furnas was ordered to retire to Baxter Springs, however, most of the Cherokee Nation was open to Confederate activity. Always mindful of the shifting balance of power, civilians followed the withdrawing Union forces.

For most of the year the action centered on the area near the Missouri and Arkansas border. Colonel Douglas Cooper, now commanding the forces of Indian Territory for the Confederacy, moved his Indian and Texan troops north and east to meet the concentration of Confederate forces. Confederate aggression caught the Second Indian Home Guard on September 20, causing panic among the fifteen hundred women and children camped with them. The Union Indians rallied, however, and drove off the enemy with twenty six casualties.[29] The Union forces of the Department of Missouri, under the field command of General John Schofield, prepared to drive the Confederates out of Missouri. The combatants met at Newtonia, Missouri, where the Union kept two of its Indian brigades with the baggage train, but sent the Third IHG under Phillips to hold the left flank.[30] These men apparently fought well in the brush and timber along a creek. By October 4, the strengthened forces of the Union drove Cooper back into Arkansas and Indian Territory, relieving the pressure on Missouri. Following the victory, Union General James Blunt moved into the Cherokee Nation and caught Cooper at Fort Wayne near the Arkansas border. The resulting skirmish pitted Indian against Indian, although the Confederate Native troops reportedly fled in the face of onrushing federal troops.[31] Cooper lost all his artillery and most of his camp in the encounter. Many of the Chickasaw and Choctaw forces had returned home. Cooper followed suit and withdrew to the Choctaw Nation. To finalize Union control of northwestern Arkansas, Blunt clashed with the Army of the Trans-Mississippi at the battle of Prairie Grove on December 7. In preparation for the engagement C.S.A. General Hindman exhorted his troops that the enemy had no sense of mercy or kindness because they were "Pin Indians."[32]

Military service for most American Indians remained a personal and Indian nation issue, not a matter of Confederate or Union loyalty. Even small skirmishes affected daily life. Stand Watie had already moved his family home to Webbers Falls, but with Blunt pushing Watie's forces back, Confederate families had to move farther south. As Watie's family fled the unrest in the nation, he and his men remained on Cherokee soil. They were drawn out to Prairie Grove, Arkansas, in December to counter a Northern offensive but soon retired to Webbers Falls for the winter. Elias C. Boudinot, Watie's nephew, traveled to Richmond to take a seat in the Confederate Congress, hoping to gain support and assistance for his Cherokee people.

CONFEDERATE REVERSALS

The Union, at least in the form of the Indian Brigade under Colonel Phillips, began to take more interest in Indian Territory. Phillips was aware of the value of staying abreast of current tensions and problems in the Confederate camp. During the winter of 1863, Phillips supported Union Cherokee efforts to hold a council at Cowskin Prairie. The council delegates, protected by Union forces, renounced the Cherokee treaty with the Confederacy and declared the nation's allegiance to the Union—a symbolic if hollow gesture considering the council's lack of authority to speak for the whole Cherokee Nation. Still, other proclamations that abolished slavery and stripped Confederate Cherokees of rights and property widened the chasm between the Cherokee factions.[33] When the northern Cherokees sent a delegation to Washington to represent their interests, the Nation as a whole seemed doomed to division.

Phillips also planned a Union show of force in Indian Territory. The refugee situation along the Kansas and Missouri borders required action. Most of the civilians who followed the Union expedition into the Cherokee and Creek Nations in 1862 had once again retreated north to the safety of Union lines. Bitter from the failure of the Federal government to recapture their homeland, and suffering through an extremely harsh winter, these Indians demanded a solution. Any invasion force intending to relocate civilian farmers had to move as soon as the grass became green enough to support livestock. In preparation, Phillips moved the Union Indian Brigade to Bentonville, Arkansas, in early March 1863. While there, smallpox swept through the camps of both refugees and soldiers, just as measles had done over the winter, revealing the continued threat of European diseases to Native peoples. Phillips proceeded cautiously, sending detachments on reconnaissance missions to probe the enemy's strength. At Park Hill they learned that Confederates wearing Federal uniforms (probably Quantrill's men) killed some Pin Cherokees.[34] The Cherokee Nation was still a volatile region. The main Union force finally crossed the Arkansas border into the Cherokee Nation on April 7, 1863, nearly a year after Weer's ill-fated expedition. The long awaited homecoming finally occurred. About one thousand families, accompanied by soldiers, made up the mile-long refugee train that snaked its way down from Neosho, Missouri. As they passed their homes many families left the train, while the remainder continued on to Park Hill.

Phillip's goal was the military installation at Fort Gibson. The fort sat on a high spot overlooking the Grand River, a few miles from its confluence with the Arkansas. The military had constructed stone storehouses which the Indian Brigade could use for supplies. The Second Indian Home Guards went in first and pushed out a company of Watie's men, thus clearing Confederate forces from the area north of the Arkansas River. The new surge of Union power called for celebration, and Colonel Phillips obliged by staging a day of festivities featuring speeches in Cherokee by officers Lewis Downing and William P. Ross.[35]

The Confederate Cherokees held no celebrations. The shift in the balance of power rippled through the area. Union troops were now in a position to repay what they viewed as injustices from previous years. Wealthy, pro-Confederate families made excellent targets. At the house of Ella Robinson, whose brother had been taken prisoner, black soldiers took food and valuables, tore open feather beds, and ransacked clothing. Eventually, all the furniture was broken and the house set ablaze by Colonel Phillips himself, despite the pleas of the women of the house. In confirmation of the new regime, all the family's slaves ran away, taking the best horses. Empty slave cabins served as the only shelter for the family who soon became refugees.[36]

As their families struggled, so too did Watie's men. They continually complained about "destitution and the inadequacy of the Confederate protection," and some expressed themselves more practically by deserting to the Union. Douglass Cooper worried that if the Confederacy did not send in well-supplied troops, the Cherokees would submit to save their nation further destruction.[37] When Stand Watie addressed his followers he spoke of "evil times" and referred to "disaster after disaster" in military operations. Their experience mirrored the disappointments of the Confederacy's western theater, and they joined the national practice of looking to the east for good news.

Although the Confederates continued to harass Federal troops and civilians, mainly through Watie's efforts, they never regained control of the Cherokee Nation. The Federal presence in Indian Territory continued to strengthen throughout the war, maintaining a permanent if tenuous hold on Fort Gibson.[38] As indicators of Watie's lack of power, a Union attack at Webbers Falls routed undressed men from a camp soon to be abandoned and also broke up a planned National Council.[39] A retaliatory attack on a wagon train ended with Watie's men scurrying back across the Arkansas River.

Confederate fortunes did not only wane in Indian Territory. The first week of July 1863 was extremely disappointing for the Confederacy. Vicksburg, Mississippi, fell to Ulysses S. Grant after a long siege in which residents were driven to the brink of starvation. Robert E. Lee's invasion of the North faltered on the bloody fields of Gettysburg, Pennsylvania. General Theophilus Holmes was badly defeated at Helena, Arkansas. And Confederate Indian forces failed to capture a Fort Gibson supply train. While Lee gambled and lost in Pennsylvania, Watie boldly attacked three hundred Federal supply wagons at Cabin Creek. If victorious, he would have gained crucial supplies while depriving Federal troops of the food necessary to hold Fort Gibson. The Federals were well prepared with howitzers and plenty of manpower, however, and succeeded in driving off the attackers.[40] The Cherokee versus Cherokee bloodshed gained nothing for the Confederates and proved to be a bitter loss for the southern effort.[41]

Two weeks later, the Confederate Indian forces lost again in the largest engagement fought in Indian Territory. Early in July, Union General James G. Blunt had taken the offensive to stop a Confederate attack on Fort Gibson. He marched his three thousand man force south, crossing the Arkansas River to meet the enemy at Honey Springs on Elk Creek, Creek Nation. Skirmishing between the two sides began on the morning of July 17, reaching a full-scale conflict by that afternoon. Douglas Cooper, in command of the Confederate Indian regiments, had a numerical advantage over Blunt that was negated by inferior ammunition. Wet gunpowder proved unreliable in firing, a problem compounded by the arrival of rain. The battle began with an artillery duel that favored the Union force because it had twelve pieces, including large Napoleons, versus the Confederates' four small mountain howitzers.[42] Similarly, Blunt's Union troops—white, black, and Indian—carried Springfield rifles or breech-loading carbines, far superior to the odd collection of various weapons carried by the Confederates.

In the two-hour exchange between infantry and dismounted cavalry, a series of blunders plagued both sides. The Second Indian Home Guards advanced in front of the Federal line, causing a lull in the firing as they fell back to proper position. Texas troops pushed hard onto what they thought was a Federal retreat, only to smash into the fierce fighting soldiers of the First Kansas Colored Infantry. The Texans' retreat triggered the collapse of the Confederate line, and Cooper ordered a withdrawal. Cooper failed to hold off Northern attacks until the arrival of reinforcements, which he finally met two hours after the battle. The victory clearly belonged to the North. Confederate Indians retreated from the field having lost several hundred dead, wounded, and captured.[43] Stand Watie's men fought without their commander, then on detached duty at Webbers Falls. Cooper believed they would have done better had Watie been present, although none of the units fought well. An eyewitness noted that one Confederate Creek regiment "did not fight but run," while another "fought awhile and then run," and the Choctaws "fought a little more" than the Creeks. Blunt declined to pursue the retreating enemy and returned to Fort Gibson.[44] Later that summer, Blunt defeated Confederate Indian forces at Perryville and Scullyville, Choctaw Nation, before returning to the safety of Fort Gibson.

As the war continued through 1863 and 1864, Indian Territory settled into a desultory routine of raids and small skirmishes. Union troops held Fort Gibson and then Fort Smith, but never truly dominated the region because Confederates continued to harass detached parties. In October 1863, Stand Watie's men raided Park Hill, burning the council house and John Ross's fine mansion Rose Cottage. The Union had similarly burned homes in Webbers Falls where Watie's supporters lived. In this and other sweeps, Watie's men also captured well-known Unionists and slaves. These forays into Union territory bolstered Confederate morale and unnerved local residents. They prevented refugees from reclaiming their farms and thus gaining independence from the army, but had little value as military offensives and would not win the war. The Confederates could not defeat the enemy because they could not draw them far from the forts.[45]

Unable to best the enemy's soldiers, the Confederate forces concentrated on attacking Federal stores. Watie's capture of provisions from the steamboat *J. R. Williams* on the Arkansas River remains a story of daring in the annals of Indian Territory warfare. The boat was running from Fort Smith to Fort Gibson in June 1864, carrying supplies intended for the Union Cherokees. It had no cavalry escort riding the banks and was thus an easy target for Watie's horsemen, themselves accompanied by three artillery pieces. A small portion of Watie's force crippled the passing steamer with a rapid volley and quickly commandeered the boat and cargo. The Indian soldiers took to celebrating their good fortune, only to learn of approaching enemy troops.[46] Captain G. W. Grayson, a young Creek officer, remembered the excitement of the attack and the honor of being chosen to guard the booty. His self-importance prevented him from painting a true picture of the situation, although he did note that he was the only Creek who would abide by the order to stand watch. Most of the poorly supplied Indian soldiers rejoiced at the availability of food, and Creeks and Seminoles promptly carried off as much booty as they could for destitute family members. The temporary desertion left Watie without enough manpower to remove the flour, bacon, and other foodstuffs that would have greatly benefited the southern forces. The loss of supplies hurt the Union but did not greatly enrich the Confederates.[47]

Watie's capture of a federal wagon train a few months later at Cabin Creek, site of his failed 1863 attempt, was more valuable. Watie's Cherokees encountered and drove off the Union Cherokees guarding the three hundred wagons of supplies bound for

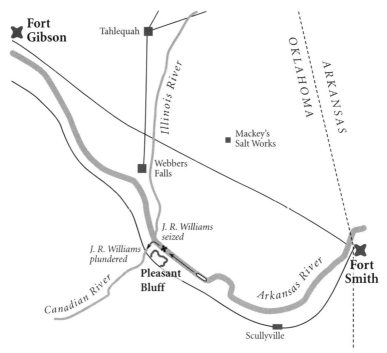

J. R. Williams attack.

Fort Smith. By a clever deception, Watie managed to slip away
with much needed supplies and avoid encountering a larger
Union relief force. One participant noted that the leaders
would not have undertaken the raid had their command not
been so destitute of clothing. This individual described himself
as dressed with a backless shirt, shoes without soles, and pants
with only the lining remaining; he was not the exception in his
command. The victorious Confederate Indian forces feasted
on Yankee food and helped themselves to enemy goods, which
many took to their refugee families. The pattern of raiding
Federal supplies also created an interesting problem of Confederate forces dressed in blue uniforms, which at times made

identification difficult.[48] Although the materials Watie took from Federal trains deprived the enemy of ammunition, clothing, food, and medical items that they desperately needed, the interruption of supplies was not enough to dislodge the United States Army from the Creek and Cherokee Nations. Overall, Watie's raids made him a legendary figure but did little to regain control of his homeland.[49]

With Federal forces occupying the major posts at Fort Gibson and Fort Smith, Confederate Indian troops made their headquarters near Boggy Depot in the Choctaw Nation. This arrangement meant long rides to scout into the Creek and Cherokee Nations. The location did succeed in placing many members of the Indian units near their families. When the Union reasserted control over northern Indian Territory in 1863, most Confederate sympathizers fled. They lived as refugees in the vicinity of the Red River, either in the Choctaw and Chickasaw Nations or in Texas. Many soldiers helped struggling families with their relocation and then continued to support them by sending food or providing occasional labor.[50]

The necessities involved in supporting families meant that Confederate Indian troops were as likely to be away visiting relatives as to be in camp. A captain returned to his unit and found the whole command "more or less dispersed throughout the country, each man of family being absorbed with [family] considerations." When Confederate Captain B. W. Marston arrived at Boggy Depot he could not inspect the Indian Division because they had "dispersed and gone to their homes." Officers knew that if the region were truly threatened by enemy attack, however, the Indian soldiers would return to headquarters.[51]

During the spring of 1864 Stand Watie received his commission as a brigadier general, making him the highest ranking Indian officer. The Confederate Indians continued to endure changes of largely white leadership, however. General Samuel Maxey took control of the southern effort in Indian Territory at the end of 1863 after General William Steele asked to be relieved.[52] The Indians generally disliked Steele, so Maxey promised a welcome change. Maxey immediately set out to reform the disorganized Indian troops.[53] His efforts breathed new life into the Confederate cause in the territory, resulting in the aforementioned raids and a general reenlistment of Indian troops. Nevertheless, the entire territory was plagued with violence, corruption, and political intrigue, and Maxey was no match for it. Douglas Cooper resented his superior and pressured Richmond to give him Maxey's command.[54] Although denied his wish for some time, Cooper finally achieved full control over Indian Territory in March 1865.[55] He found himself in charge of a dying cause. Just three months later, General Edward Kirby Smith surrendered the Trans-Mississippi Department to Union General Edward R. S. Canby. The military experiment of separate Indian units fighting under their own national identities ended, never to be repeated.

CHAPTER 4

Cherokees in Service
and at Home

*This morn. we saw the Southern army pass, on the very same
road where, exactly a week before, we had watched the Federals
pass . . . What next will we see?*

HANNAH HICKS

CHEROKEES AS SOLDIERS

The Indian units left a unique legacy, generating both positive
and negative reactions. The armies of both sides accepted
Indian soldiers reluctantly, and perhaps never fully appreciated
their service. Although the Confederacy embraced the idea of
Indian allies at an early stage, diplomats in Richmond, not commanders in the field, saw advantages to Native military participation.
The decision to use Indian assistance was not necessarily supported
by line officers. Field experience reinforced negative perceptions
among some commanders but prompted positive evaluations
from others.

Negative images often focused on barbarity and cruelty. One
of the earliest encounters of the war produced such negative
reports. Texas troops recorded that Creeks scalped other Indians
at the battle of Chusto-Talasah and regarded this as an indication of the hatred between rival national factions. The battle of
Pea Ridge prompted another notable public debate over the

94

supposed propensity of Indian troops to act in an uncivilized manner. When the Union victors collected their dead and wounded at Pea Ridge, they claimed to have found evidence of "barbarity."[1] Witnesses attested that Iowa soldiers were scalped and their necks pierced with long knives. The Iowans' strongly held opinions that this was the work of Indians quickly fanned public indignation. The *New York Tribune* accused Albert Pike of leading an "Aboriginal Corps of Tomahawkers and Scalpers" at Pea Ridge. The behavior of Cherokees accused of scalping and mutilating the Federal dead even came before the Joint Committee on the Conduct of the War. The Confederacy showed little inclination to stand behind its allies in putting down this talk of barbarism.[2] General Van Dorn declined to comment officially about any Indian participation in the battle. He did respond to the Union's claim, however, by stating that he hoped the reports were erroneous because "the Indians who formed part of his forces having for many years been regarded as civilized people." He then ended the exchange with a counterclaim alleging that Germans had murdered Confederate prisoners in cold blood.[3]

Scalping appalled white sensibilities. Army officers, whose duty demanded inflicting death and suffering on the enemy, purported to be outraged by this behavior. That whites had long paid a bounty for Indian scalps during warfare, dating at least to the French efforts against the Chickasaws, never entered the discussion.[4] It is obvious to modern scholars that such pronouncements of barbarism are based in cultural norms. Native troops merely acted according to their own traditions. They were, however, aware of white officials' distaste for such activity and occasionally promised to desist. The Cherokee National Council sought to ward off accusations of cruelty and scalping through a plea to its members to conduct war on the basis of "humane principles." It should be noted, however, that Native troops were not the only combatants practicing barbarism in the Civil War. Warfare in the trans-Mississippi West has been described as "war to the knife and the knife to the hilt." Numerous accounts of inhumane behavior, including scalping, characterize white actions in the west. Most tales of Indian atrocities seem minor in comparison to the conduct of Jayhawkers and guerrillas such as Quantrill and Anderson.[5]

Charges of barbarism stemmed from the racist belief that Indians were uncivilized and inferior. Indian soldiers faced an incredible amount of racism from white officers.[6] Colonel Charles DeMorse unapologetically stated his firmly held opinion that "the Indian is physiologically recognized as an inferior race." He added, "No Indian is qualified by attainments for such duty as regulations of the army call for," due to the "well-known incapacity of that people to direct operations which require promptness and concentration of mind." DeMorse's attitude reflected a stereotype of the perpetually late, inherently lazy, dull-witted Native person. Unfortunately, his views were probably not remarkable among white officers.[7] Many white officers had no intention of serving under Native officers.[8] DeMorse couched his refusal to enter into such a situation in terms he surely believed were rational. "It is an obvious trait of the Indian's character that those people are naturally indisposed, as well as unfitted, to lead and of their own impulses always prefer to be led and to repose upon the judgment and superior mental acuteness of the white man."[9] Stand Watie and many other Native leaders surely would have disagreed.

Many white officers and enlisted men believed that innate inferiority rendered Indians poor soldiers. General William Steele represented the views many white commanders had of Native soldiers when he described Indians as "wholly unreliable as troops of the line." The main complaint seemed to be that Indians did not follow orders and generally disregarded military procedure. Even their primary champion, Albert Pike, announced that "Indian troops are of course entirely undisciplined."[10] Not surprisingly, the issue of discipline caused the most friction between Indian troops and white officials, and even Indian officers were regarded as "indisposed to enforce discipline." One evaluation charged Indian troops with being "almost as destitute of every attribute of a soldier as if they were raw recruits." The same charges could be leveled at any green recruits in either army, and Indian troops never received extensive training to alter their concepts of proper military behavior.

Much of the antipathy toward Indian soldiers came from a lack of understanding between the two cultures. Rank-and-file Native troops rarely drilled or fought as units in the manner of white and black soldiers, nor was there any reason to assume they would have.[11] Troops were poorly armed and frequently thrown into regiments without military training. Despite considerable assimilation, men from the Five Nations came from a much different background than the average Union or Confederate soldier. As boys they grew up admiring great warriors such as Tecumseh or Red Eagle more than George Washington or Andrew Jackson. The glory and honor that accrued to Native leaders did not come from enduring a hard winter at Valley Forge. It came through quick, decisive raids that accomplished their objective and returned as many unscathed men as possible to their families. Thus it made little sense to Indians to remain in winter quarters with the knowledge that there would likely be no fighting until spring, or to line up and march across a field toward the enemy when nearby trees provided life-saving cover. Indian troops signed up to defend their homes, not to build huts and wait out the winter away from their families. Consequently, orders to assemble in camps had little effect except to frustrate white officers.[12]

Another major complaint about Native units focused on deficient paperwork. The military functioned on endless inspections, rosters, and reports, but it proved amazingly difficult to get such communication from the commands in Indian Territory. Indian officers ignored this duty for a variety of reasons that probably included the tedium of paperwork, illiteracy, lack of supplies, and a general disregard for the importance of records in a traditionally oral culture.[13]

Not all white officers had negative impressions of their Indian soldiers, however. Albert Pike and Douglas Cooper, each of whom had experience with Native culture and allowed the men to fight as they wished, fared much better in their relations with the troops than outsiders such as William Steele.[14] Even some of those new to Indian commands had positive experiences. Samuel Maxey recognized that by treaty the Indian troops could not be required to fight outside their homeland, and he was most grateful for their efforts. Experience convinced him of the wisdom of using the men in raids, although his Indian soldiers still spent considerable time guarding supply lines and securing provisions rather than fighting.[15] Finally, Maxey firmly supported the equality of Native officers with white officers when challenged with the idea that whites would not serve under Indians.[16]

Indian troops left observers with solid impressions, whether positive or negative. Many whites commented on the unique whooping sounds made by Native troops in battle. Union officers at Neosho, Missouri, blamed the screaming and whooping of the Indians for rendering their horses almost unmanageable. Wiley Britton, who often fought with Union Indian troops, recalled the war whoop that resonated through the woods when the Indian units were underway. He described a "yelping" that lasted fifteen or twenty minutes. Indian soldiers often complemented such characteristic noises with traditional war paint. This traditional behavior was meant both to embolden the Indians and terrorize the enemy.[17] Britton noticed that whites were afraid of the Indian soldiers, but he also noted that the fear was due to the Indians' strange appearance and not their behavior. He reported that Indian troops marching and camping in Arkansas did not molest anyone in their homes. Indeed, Native soldiers were rarely charged with pillaging or similar activities.[18] Many whites would have been surprised to learn that men regarded as "savages" often behaved better than white soldiers.

Regardless of how whites viewed them as soldiers, Indian troops received poor treatment. Neither the Union nor the Confederacy adequately supplied its Indian allies. Lack of food, clothing, and arms prompted the most complaints from officers and enlisted men in Indian units. Every officer who took command found his Native troops lacking even basic weapons. More than one thousand soldiers had no arms at all in the Confederate Indian regiments in 1863.[19] Commanders went to great lengths to procure suitable supplies, only to have them preempted by white units. Albert Pike spent most of his time in command attempting to arm and clothe his Indian troops. When he did manage to assemble clothing and tents, the items were often taken by white commands. When General Van Dorn retreated from Pea Ridge his men plundered the supplies intended for Confederate Indian soldiers, so that almost no full boxes arrived in Indian Territory. Union Indian troops fared similarly, never receiving the quality of weaponry used by their white counterparts. One observer referred to the guns issued to Indian recruits as "antiquated." Indians who joined the army could expect to go without food or blankets.[20] Even appeals by the chiefs themselves failed to rectify the supply situation in Indian Territory. Furthermore, as with most Civil War units, no Indian commands received pay with any regularity, and most were owed more than a year of back pay.[21]

Such conditions gave Indian allies on both sides ample cause to abandon their wartime allegiance. Desertion certainly occurred among Indian units. Drew's men provide the most obvious example, yet all did not withdraw from the war; many simply switched sides in mid-contest. Stand Watie pointed with great pride to the loyalty of his men in the midst of hardship, claiming a lower number of desertions than other similar commands.

Indeed, General Maxey praised the efforts of his Indian cavalry and described the demoralization of white units outdoing each other in the number of desertions recorded. On the other hand, Cherokees and Creeks left the Union invasion force of 1862 in droves.[22]

Conditions on the home front and relationships between soldiers and their commanders contributed to the frequency of desertion. Men from both armies left military camps to help refugee families relocate, plant or harvest crops, or gather supplies. Most had enlisted to protect their homelands, and ensuring the survival of families was surely part of that commitment. Indian soldiers retained an independence unrivaled by white troops. If they did not like the direction or focus of higher command they did not comply. White officers who led the Union Indian brigade into the Cherokee Nation in 1862 failed to achieve the soldiers' goal of regaining their homes; therefore, the soldiers left the service. This did not mean they would not fight again, only that they no longer believed in the current efforts. On the Confederate side, Albert Pike spent two valuable days paying his Choctaw and Chickasaw regiments before they would agree to march to Pea Ridge, and even then they only showed up after the battle.[23]

The records of the Indian troops in both armies are incomplete, but each year's returns listed hundreds of Native soldiers as deserters. For example, an analysis of the compiled service records of the First, Second, and Third Indian Home Guards shows an average of 18 percent desertion, although that obscures the 26 percent rate for the First IHG. Although the military judged Indian soldiers by its own definition of desertion or official leave, existing records suggest that perhaps the idea of desertion was open to interpretation. Indian soldiers did not come from a culture dependent on papers and official forms. Indeed, many of the more traditional men did not read or write English. If families needed them or camp life became onerous, they were not conditioned to think of filing an official form granting permission to leave. They simply went away and came back later. What the army regarded as desertion, the men thought of as a long furlough. This phenomenon also occurred in white Confederate units.[24]

The records of the Indian Home Guard reveal a pattern of coming and going from army camps. Muster rolls were completed sporadically, but they reflect a constantly fluctuating body. Artishomity, for example, enlisted in the First Indian Home Guard in April 1862, was declared absent without leave by August, noted present again in November, and then deserted in February. Cashdoyoulsots from the Third Indian Home Guard was listed as deserted four times in less than two years. Many men probably did not understand the consequences of staying away from camp too long. Numerous individuals applied for pensions after the war, not realizing that they had been declared deserters. The service record of Kumsey Yahola lists him as a three-time deserter. He was gone for months, but he believed he had done no more than remain a little too long on his furlough, admitting on his pension application that previously he had been home "a time or two" to see his parents. Chesqukerlooyar received a furlough after an illness, delayed his return to take care of his family, and was consequently listed as a deserter. Other sources of miscommunication grew out of the tendency of Indians to rely on relatives or locals for help rather than the army. Watt Cochran became ill at Cabin Creek and was taken home by his brother, but he did not have official leave. Runabout Proctor also did not report to the military for medical help, preferring to rely on a Cherokee doctor to care for his wound. These men may have been enlisted soldiers, but nothing in their background would cause them to rely on military organization or white medical systems for help. Because these soldiers fought near home and could rely on civilian aid, they fell out of the military reporting system.[25]

Misunderstandings did not account for all desertions in the Indian regiments. Many men left military service willfully. Such unreliability constantly frustrated officers who expected some semblance of military discipline. One officer was driven to remark on a young Cherokee's record: "If there is no Hell there should be one made for this villian more fierce than the multiplied furies of the infernal reageous. Deserted time & again to give dates would be a stigima on all officers that ever had anything to do with the Company." Disgusted by the character of this soldier, the officer listed the man's occupation as "horse thief."[26]

Most Indian enlistees were neither model soldiers nor incorrigible rogues. They served their time in the military participating in a few battles, taking part in raids, and trying to relieve the boredom in camps. As was true of all Civil War soldiers, the Indians' worst enemy was disease. Typhoid fever and smallpox, for which few Indians were vaccinated, ravaged both military and civilian settlements, resulting in high mortality rates. Shortages of supplies and the general dearth of food in Indian country weakened many through malnutrition, leaving them more susceptible to diseases. Although it was not glorious to die in a hospital, it remained far more common than death on the battlefield. Twice as many white soldiers died of disease as were killed in battle, and the toll for Indian troops was at least as high.[27]

Native Americans in Indian Territory endured a negative military experience in the Civil War. The problems they faced both reflected and diverged from those of more mainstream soldiers. Feelings of loneliness and boredom in camp, interspersed with terror and discomfort in the field, were common to all men in uniform.[28] Inadequate supplies furnished to Native units compounded the usual hardships, and the men saw little actual fighting to relieve the monotony. The nature of warfare in Indian Territory exacerbated the difficulties hared with other soldiers. The Cherokees had to face fellow tribal members in the conflict, making it more difficult to dehumanize the enemy.

Years of being the "other" in American society forged a sense of commonality that almost certainly affected the psychological aspect of combat. Above all, military experience left Indian soldiers destitute and unappreciated, with little to show for their efforts. Their contributions were quickly forgotten by white politicians, and Indian veterans returned home to societies rendered nearly unrecognizable because of the combined pressures of guerrilla warfare and waves of refugees.

CIVILIANS

As Cherokee men and boys struggled with the realities of military service, their families faced their own difficulties in the nation. More so than most United States civilians, inhabitants of Indian Territory became intimately acquainted with the horrors of warfare. Most northerners could conduct their daily business without interruption by the war, and few outside Pennsylvania or Maryland endured the invasion of their homeland by enemy troops or the extreme shortages of goods brought on by wartime conditions. Even most southern states feared only the arrival of the Union army. The situation in the Cherokee Nation, however, resembled that of lower border state Missouri, the horrors of which have been well documented.[29]

The first concerted military action of the Civil War in Indian Territory, Confederate pursuit of Opothleyahola's group in 1861, was an act of warfare primarily aimed against civilians. This established a trend that continued throughout the war. The Union army, the Confederate army, Jayhawkers, bushwhackers, William Clarke Quantrill's band, and numerous other outlaws frequented the region, producing a volatile and dangerous situation for combatants and residents alike. Those who joined the armies of the contending nations naturally faced hardships and the possibility of death, but those who remained at home dealt with an equally uncertain future. Murder, theft, shortage of food, inadequate medical aid, and a lack of transportation and communication combined to challenge civilians in Indian Territory.

The crisis in Indian Territory immediately affected white persons living in the Five Nations. Only a small number of whites legally resided in any Indian nation.[30] Intermarried whites, a few traders, and Christian missionaries constituted the majority of whites in Indian country. The small but dedicated missionary presence in Indian Territory consisted of men and women who chose to serve the Indian nations, often for their entire lives. Well acquainted with one another, a few families intermarried and thus tightened the bonds in the community.[31] This literate group, educated in eastern schools, left more diaries and letters than the people to whom they preached Christianity. They shared their lives with Native peoples, and some recorded the wartime conditions experienced by Indian Territory civilians. Missionaries to the Five Nations remained committed to their positions within the church, but found their work halted as schools and churches closed and physical harm loomed. Interruptions in daily routine varied from minor annoyances to serious upheavals. An unknown person murdered Moravian missionary William Ward while he searched for his cow in the woods. The Federal Army arrested another Moravian, the Reverend Gilbert Bishop, and although he was quickly released the incident proved unnerving. Like Gilbert, who moved his family to Philadelphia soon after his detainment, many missionaries fled the Indian nations. They traveled north and east to return to families or visit friends for the duration of the war, keeping in touch with Indian Territory via infrequent letters.[32]

The family of prominent missionary Samuel Worcester belonged to the Cherokee Nation in the way that mattered most to the Indians—they chose to live among them and share their lives. Worcester's daughters grew up, taught, and lived in the nation. Hannah Worcester married Abijah Hicks, a Cherokee, in 1852, and thereafter lived in the sometimes conflicting worlds of whites and Cherokees. Her missionary friends joined the exodus of whites from the territory, but most Native people could not easily relocate. Hannah's family stayed in Park Hill and shared the fate of their Cherokee relatives. The diary Hannah kept provides historians with a fascinating window on home life in the Cherokee Nation. As a young mother, Hannah worried as her support system of friends and sisters left the territory for a life she acknowledged as safer than her own. She watched as husband Abijah prepared the wagon that would take her sister Ann Eliza Robertson and family away from Park Hill.[33] With the flight of trusted friends and relatives, Hannah's Christian faith and dedication to her own family would have to see her through the upcoming challenges.[34]

The distress of a country torn by civil divisions shattered daily life in the Cherokee Nation. Existence grew more precarious, regardless of one's sectional leanings, as tensions between Cherokee factions rose and violence increased. The extended family of Samuel Worcester, like many of his colleagues, maintained Unionist sympathies. This could be either a curse or a blessing depending on the shifting balance of power. It was never a guarantee of safety. Alliances and any sense of security they might have conveyed constantly changed. A Pin Indian, who should have been an ally, murdered Abijah Hicks, possibly mistaking him for another man.[35] That the murder may have been a mistake certainly gave little comfort to Hicks's young wife, who as a missionary was shocked by Abijah's lonely death forty miles from home without a proper Christian burial. Pro-Union Cherokees also burned a home owned by Hannah in order to punish the resident, Abijah's brother-in-law Spencer Stephens. Spencer was targeted by Pins as a Confederate supporter, though he later served in the Union Indian regiment.[36]

Divisions emerged even within the close-knit community of missionaries. Guided by their faith in Christian teachings and the experience of minority status in an Indian nation, the missionaries attempted to stand by one another. Hannah noted sorrowfully the murders of various teachers and preachers, who fell prey to the lawlessness in the Cherokee Nation. Yet she also expressed relief when the Reverend Stephen Foreman left the nation. Foreman was a mixed-blood Cherokee whose bilingual ability proved invaluable to the American Board. He lived with Samuel Worcester during his pursuit of a theological education and later served as his assistant. Under Worcester's tutelage, Foreman forged an important link between white missionaries and their Native constituents. In 1861, Foreman supported the South and vocally criticized other missionaries for their Unionist sympathies. He turned to them for help, however, when he felt threatened by the power of the loyal Cherokees. Hannah Hicks ignored rumors that connected Foreman to her husband's death, risking retaliation by hiding Foreman from the Pins. Foreman moved his family farther south in 1862 when tension increased and communities further divided, eventually living as a refugee in Sulphur Springs, Texas. This situation reflected the reality that missionaries brought much cultural baggage to their positions. They formed opinions influenced by regional upbringing, personal experience, and personality. Although representing their churches, on issues as emotional as civil war even missionaries operated as individuals.[37]

Conditions in the Cherokee Nation were so volatile that it did not require provocative actions to get in trouble. Residents attempted to avoid the pervasive looting, pillaging, and murdering by remaining as inconspicuous as possible. Daniel Dwight Hitchcock, widower of Hannah's sister, suffered capture by the Confederates for admitting his preference for the Union. A son of northern missionaries, Hitchcock perhaps naturally favored the Union, but there is little evidence that he actively espoused the cause or threatened Confederate control. Confederate Colonel Douglas Cooper implied that he held Hitchcock for his own safety due to "the state of feeling in the country." Perhaps Cooper genuinely cared about Hitchcock's fate; more likely, he was considered to be a harmful influence as an educated, well-respected figure who might voice opposition to Confederate alliance. This minor military decision affected the lives of dozens of civilians in the Park Hill area who depended on Hitchcock as their only physician.[38]

Any indication that an individual did not support the cause invited violence from Confederates. Isaac Hitchcock, brother of Daniel, appears to have been outspoken in his negative opinions of the Confederacy. Isaac's hired hand left his employ, citing the danger of living with a northern man and threatening to report him as such to Fort Smith, "which is the same as a man's death warrant." Isaac was reported as a missionary and an abolitionist, a common association regardless of its validity. The situation was so tense that a drunken man accused Hitchcock of being a spy simply because he received a letter with a Washington, D.C., postmark. Travel became dangerous for men who, like Hitchcock, had chosen not to join the army. Conscription into the military might result from a trip to get supplies. Isaac Hitchcock consciously avoided areas and roads where Stand Watie's men traveled. More than once he was unwillingly pressed into temporary service as a soldier.[39]

Rejecting military duty was not a popular choice in Indian Territory. Nancy Jane Rider's father "did not believe in fighting" and did not enlist. He paid a high price for his defiance. Along with others who did not enlist, he remained in seclusion for the duration of the war, hiding in the dense woods, sleeping in caves, and subsisting on wild game and meager food supplies smuggled to them by their families. Men who had already run into trouble with the enemy found it difficult to return home because of the possibility of being surprised by troops. Daniel

Dwight Hitchcock's mother rejoiced at his release and return home, only to fear for his life a few days later when Confederate forces passed by her farm.[40]

Residents of Indian Territory attempting to escape the insecure life at home had several options. They could look for employment elsewhere, as Isaac Hitchcock did by teaching school in Kansas. Men could join either army and hope for at least the basic necessities of life from the military. Women naturally had fewer choices than men. Many families followed fathers and husbands into the army, often ending up in refugee camps. Hannah's sister-in-law, Sarah Stephens, left Park Hill with the Union army and joined thousands of other refugees at Neosho, Missouri. But relocation frequently did not represent a viable choice. Women, especially those with husbands who had been killed or were away, often did not have the means to leave home. Like Hannah Hicks, they had to find a way to survive and hold their families together.

For much of the war, Cherokees lived in an occupied terri-tory. Before the war, the Cherokee Nation existed as an almost autonomous entity, providing its own legislature, judicial system, and law enforcement. Federal presence was limited to small garrisons in a few forts intended to protect "civilized" Indians from "uncivilized" tribes. Fort Gibson had been decommis-sioned and federal troops withdrawn; thus the arrival of various military units in the Cherokee Nation represented a drastic change. From 1862 to 1864, the opposing forces contended for control of northeastern Indian Territory. Confederates could never completely hold the area north of the Arkansas River, nor could the Federals secure it. The contested region included both the Cherokee national capital at Tahlequah and the residential area of some of the nation's wealthiest citizens at Park Hill. The Confederate Cherokee forces under the command of Stand Watie naturally desired to control this important area, both for its strategic value and because John Ross and many of his supporters had homes there. Similarly, Park Hill figured in the plans of the Federal forces attempting to reestablish dominance in the Cherokee Nation.[41]

The first attempt of the Union to gain control of the Park Hill area in 1862 ended in failure, creating unrest and confusion. The departure of the military left civilians without a leader. When John Ross was spirited away by Federal troops in July, the people of Park Hill and Tahlequah lost the focus of the community. Ross had been both a political leader and a social and economic power in the area since removal. There were other officials and powerful men, but Ross kept the reins of government close and few could match his influence. Many prominent leaders who joined the Union Army could not remain in the area for fear of Confederate harassment. Cherokees who supported the Confederate cause denounced the old leadership and elected a southern Cherokee government, most of whose members served with their new chief, Stand Watie.[42] Because Watie's men traveled extensively during their military activities, they often did not reside in the nation. With neither pro-Union nor pro-Confederate leaders in the area, civilians of the Cherokee Nation were left to their own devices. Women and children made up the majority of the remaining residents. They faced numerous challenges due to wartime conditions in addition to the normal burdens of nineteenth-century life in a rural area. The uncertainty of supplies, threats of hostile raids, and isolation caused by poor communications were magnified by the conflict.

Cherokee citizens endured two armies and numerous outlaws within their nation, as well as the resulting violence and hardships. Guerrilla raiders such as Quantrill rode through the nation with impunity, and regiments or fragments of commands might show up with little or no warning. Indian civilians suffered many of the same problems that white Confederates endured in occupied areas of the South. As historian Stephen Ash has noted, mobility in occupied areas was critically curtailed by the uncertainties of travel. Civilians journeying for supplies or visits might find themselves on the road with several hundred soldiers or accompanied by a rough band of thieves. This was especially alarming for women, who generally moved about without male companionship during the war.[43]

The uncertainty of mobility greatly restricted the lives of civilians and forced an even greater self-reliance on solitary farming communities. Formerly simple tasks such as taking wheat to a mill or visiting friends became anxious trips undertaken only through necessity. With two armies on the move, accompanied by the usual shirkers, no one was safe. Everyone had heard stories of travelers such as Abijah Hicks who never came home. David Palmer, a friend of the Hicks family, made a remarkable escape with a bullet in his leg after being ambushed on the road by bushwhackers and watching his companion get shot in the head. Returning home safely proved little consolation for Palmer. In two weeks of recuperation, he ate only one meal in the house for fear of capture by Southern forces.[44]

Lack of transportation also limited travel. Almost every serviceable horse in the area, and some less sound, found its way into military service. Dr. Hitchcock's horse, Teasle, saw action with both the Union and Confederate armies. Apparently not pleased with military treatment, Teasle made periodic trips home, only to be picked up again on the next sweep. Ownership rights made little difference to those conscripting horses and mules. After Isaac Hitchcock's horse was stolen, he borrowed a neighbor's to finish plowing, only to have that horse, too, taken off to haul cannon.[45] Failing to hide a horse during a raid doomed residents to walk for the rest of the war. Imagine the frustration of Hannah Hicks when she found her horse shot in her own pasture.[46]

Home became the only refuge for civilians who could not travel safely. In many cases even the situation there was dire.

Living off the land, armies stripped the countryside as they went, bivouacking in fields, burning fences, and trampling crops. After a few encounters, civilians knew what to expect from their temporary neighbors. In 1862 Hannah Hicks noticed Confederates camped one-half mile from her farm and expected to lose her livestock. The situation in Indian Territory differed from much of the South because many soldiers from both sides lived in the region. Confederate Cherokee troops occasionally patrolled the Park Hill vicinity. This gave rise to situations where Confederate Cherokee soldiers "requisitioned" supplies from loyal Cherokees they had known all their lives. Through their involvement in churches and schools, mission families knew many local people. Thus Hannah knew the Confederates who arrived at her house to demand dinner in December 1862, and she received civil treatment from most of them.[47] The dispensing of hospitality, even in strained circumstances, was ingrained in Native culture, and most Indian Territory residents did their best to cope with the situation. Locals forced to travel would stop and stay at the homes of acquaintances regardless of whether anyone was home. Sharing resources with relatives and other tribal members remained a tradition, although it was strained by wartime changes.

It could be difficult to act equitably during war, however. Old grudges and animosities often surfaced, and resentment or jealousy of material success produced vindictive destruction or theft.[48] Theft may have been the most widespread and most difficult feature of army occupation. Those who were armed knew that they could easily take what they desired from others. Restraining soldiers from looting and pillaging easy targets required strong leadership based on allegiance, discipline, and superior power. Indian societies did not produce that type of leadership or followers, nor did many white leaders achieve it themselves. Anarchy reigned in much of the region.

Women remaining at home could expect to see at any time armed parties of men. Word usually spread through a neighborhood about impending raids, but little could be done to prevent or prepare for them. Residents might try to hide valuables if given enough advance warning. Possessions that could be buried in a yard or hidden in the hollow of a tree were those that had value in peacetime, such as china or silverware, but little worth in the daily life of war torn Indian Territory. Few women sought to impress callers with their best luxury items any longer. Valued goods in 1862 were those that kept the household functioning—oxen, pigs, home furnishings, and stored food—and did not lend themselves to easy concealment. In November 1862, soldiers robbed Hannah Hicks of nearly everything she owned. Apparently having ample time for the task, the men thoroughly ransacked every closet, drawer, trunk, and box they could find. Perhaps most infuriating for Hannah, the Cherokee leaders of the group often had dined at her home. Hannah believed that a missionary's wife directed the looters to her house, reflecting the bitter division of friends and acquaintances. In her case, fortunately, word reached Confederate General James Marmaduke, who in turn ordered a halt to the thievery and the return of some items. Although grateful for the reprieve, Hannah grieved for the loss of so many valued items. Having lost her husband and her first home, she now was forced to surrender treasured mementos as well.[49] In all, Hannah endured five robberies during the war, losing a little more each time.

Hannah's experience certainly was not unique. She recorded her shock and sorrow at the destruction of friends' homes throughout the nation as she passed ransacked houses that once offered hospitality. Numerous survivors recalled the frequent robberies of the period. Dozens of residents reported "losing everything," or mentioned that raiders "took anything they wanted." Some recorded that the thieves ransacked their house while they watched. Little could be done by women and children to stop the violence of an armed gang of men. Few received a reprieve from the thefts as did Hannah Hicks. In many cases the destruction was total: all furnishings, clothing, and structures were stolen or went up in smoke.[50]

Although the loss of personal possessions struck deep chords with women, the theft of food and livestock proved a far more serious threat to their existence. Soldiers and bushwhackers methodically stripped Indian Territory of its richest resource—livestock.[51] The soldiers ran off all of Hannah's cattle, although many of the beasts escaped and returned home. Texas troops slaughtered one ox out of each of her three trained pairs. A similar story was repeated across the nation. Women spent laborious hours breaking wild cattle to work, only to have them stolen for food. Few people could replace the pilfered animals. The loss of animals meant a corresponding lack of protein in civilian diets, and the removal of draft animals effectively halted large-scale agriculture. Otherwise stripped of much of their meat supply, residents of Indian Territory attempted to hold one or two overlooked cows or the hogs that generally ran wild until needed. The shortage of breadstuffs also reached crisis proportions. Soldiers helped themselves to grains and corn in barns and cribs. Replacing that stored food became increasingly difficult. Several of the local mills fell under military control or were destroyed. Residents found themselves traveling farther under dangerous conditions to have their few crops processed.[52]

More alarmingly, agricultural production dropped precipitately as the war continued. With men and draft animals gone and fields and fences destroyed by passing troops, women struggled to grow food. Confederates took all the stored wheat from the Ballard family in the Cherokee Nation, leaving them nothing but seed wheat. Such a loss generally forced families to eat the seed, and thus left no means to plant a crop in the following year. The situation became more desperate as each month passed.

Union Colonel William A. Phillips attempted to alleviate the worst suffering by sending trainloads of flour to civilian areas such as Park Hill. Kindhearted people such as Hannah found it difficult to refuse requests for help, but any food spared was literally taken from the mouths of her own children. By the spring of 1863, Hannah Hicks could not sustain her own family. The daughter of missionaries who had so often helped those in need now relied on what flour she was given to feed her children. Hannah noted in her diary the impending starvation of the people.[53]

Residents had trouble covering their bodies as well as sustaining them. Clothing became scarce when poorly supplied troops ransacked homes for garments, and raw materials for weaving were no longer available. Friends outside the territory sent clothing to help those left behind, but it was never enough. The Cherokee Nation in northeastern Indian Territory experienced bitter winter winds and snow accumulation that foretold hardships for those without shoes and blankets. With no access to a shoemaker, Hannah attempted to fashion cloth shoes for herself. A lack of adequate clothing may have led to increased sickness and death from exposure.[54]

Illness presented another challenge for Indian people in the territory. In the many single-parent households, an ailing adult could mean disaster for several children. Along with the constant illness of her youngest child, Hannah herself had frequent bouts of sickness. During these times she acknowledged her inability to care for her children, but there was no one else to do so. Her diary, written for her sister's information, records the deaths of many friends and relatives. Diseases such as smallpox remained problematic for Native people in this period, especially in military camps and forts where men gathered in large numbers. Soldiers who survived the close confinement and unsanitary conditions of army camps might return home to find that their family had succumbed to the harshness of civilian life. John Hicks lost two children and his mother in the first year of the war, while he and his brothers were away serving with the Federal army.[55] The unreliability of communication added to the grief caused by frequent deaths. Reports of deaths often arrived woefully late or were incorrect, increasing the emotional burden. Isolated from the rest of the country by distance and poor communication, residents of Indian Territory often wished for news of the larger conflict. The lack of accurate information about the movements of the armies frustrated civilians. Their hopes were alternately buoyed or dashed by conflicting reports of battles and skirmishes. Though frequently incorrect, reports that the enemy would arrive in the neighborhood shortly kept everyone upset and anxious. Such alarms disrupted the pattern of everyday life and made it difficult to plan for the future.[56]

Hannah Hicks and her relatives were representative of hundreds of other families caught in a crisis that changed their lives. These noncombatants lived in a constant state of anxiety for the safety and survival of their families. Everything became scarce—food, transportation, medical treatment, community life. Virtually helpless to alter the situation, women and children and a few old and ill men carried on as best they could. The majority failed. Throughout the nations livestock was stolen, crops ruined, and homes and possessions destroyed. As men returned from service in either the Union or Confederate armies they found they possessed little more than the meager clothes on their backs. Coming home often meant starting over.

CHAPTER 5

Refugees

I do wish one could have peace once more, but I fear that is not for me to see in my day.

MRS. SARAH WATIE

Those who remained in the nation made up only part of the Cherokee civilian experience. Countless families were forced to flee despite valiant efforts to remain at home. The first year of the war put Union sympathizers at risk in the Cherokee Nation. The tribe's alliance with the Confederacy, the arming of two Confederate Cherokee military units, and the enthusiasm of Colonel Cooper for the Southern cause made Union adherence an uncomfortable position. The Cherokee Nation was both a rural southern community and a tribal one. Many relationships bound the members, including extended families, clans, churches, and traditions of hospitality. The society had been divided for over two decades into rival political camps closely tied to family affiliation. Everyone would know, or presume, one's allegiance in the current conflict. When the military activity began in the nation late in 1861, Unionists faced trouble. With feelings running high and the Confederate Army on the move, some people left their homes and became refugees.

The followers of Creek traditional leader Opothleyahola became the first large group of refugees from Indian Territory. Individuals fleeing unrest in their nations migrated to the protection of this large gathering.[1] At least some of these early refugees were Cherokees; indeed, one of the leaders working with Opothleyahola, James McDaniel, was described as a "refugee Cherokee Chief."[2] As the turmoil in their nation continued, more and more Cherokees found themselves outside their nation as refugees. The story of the refugees from Indian Territory is confusing and jumbled. It involves the army and the Indian office, as well as Kansas, Missouri and the Cherokee Nation, and often fails to differentiate between among tribal identities. Much of the general description of Native refugees applies to Cherokee citizens. It is an unrelenting tale of hardship and suffering.

Refugees are defined as "persons who flee to a foreign country or power to escape danger or persecution."[3] Such people rarely have a chance to prepare for the drastic change in their life, nor do they expect an extended separation from their homes. Their dislocation often comes in a nightmarish rush when difficult choices are made under intense pressure. When the first fighting broke out in Indian Territory in 1861, civilians panicked and abandoned possessions in a desperate effort to reach safety. People threw away anything that encumbered their flight, giving little consideration to the long-term value of the blankets and clothing left behind. Cultural and personal values often outweighed practical concerns. A decision made by a woman to discard a bag of gold but retain precious turtle shell dance rattles reflected the immediacy of decisions to be made. Witnesses asserted that in the tremendous confusion mothers abandoned babies on the roadside.[4] Thousands of civilians who left most of their personal wealth behind at the beginning of a journey subsequently lost the few items they were able to transport. In the words of one man, this flight was "almost another trail of tears."[5] The agent in Kansas reported, "Families who in their country had been wealthy, and who could count their cattle by the thousands and horses by hundreds, and owned large numbers of slaves, and who at home, had lived at ease and comfort, were without even the necessaries of life."[6] Those who evaded capture by Confederate Indian forces were now displaced and destitute.

The headlong flight carried thousands of loyal Indians across the northern border of Indian Territory into Kansas.[7] Torn by recent internal civil strife, Kansas seemed an unlikely prospect for a safe haven. For refugees with few alternatives, however, it represented the comparative security of Union lines. New arrivals came under the sometimes indifferent care of the various Indian agents assigned to the tribes of Indian Territory. Southern Superintendent William Coffin ordered his new agents to meet the refugees at Fort Roe on the Verdigris River. This was the first time most agents met their Indian charges, as none had established offices in Indian Territory. Agent George A. Cutler had "deemed it unsafe to go any further [into Indian Territory]" and so returned to the safety of Washington, Fort Leavenworth, and LeRoy, Kansas, while his Creek wards fought for their existence.[8]

Those who remained were horrified by what they found, and the government agents struggled to convey the enormity of the disaster to others. Phrases such as, "It would be impossible to give an adequate description of the suffering endured," or, "I doubt much if history records an instance of sufferings equal to these," were characteristic reports from the field. Sent to observe the refugee camps in February 1862, Army surgeon A. B. Campbell had this to report:

It is impossible for me to depict the wretchedness of their condition. the only protection from the snow upon which they lie is prairie grass, and from the wind and weather scraps and rags which did not conceal their nakedness, and I saw 7 varying in age from 3–15 years without a thread upon their bodies. . . . They are extremely destitute of cooking utensils and axes or hatchets; many can with difficulty get wood to make fires, either to warm themselves or to cook with, which compels many to eat their provision almost raw. . . . They greatly need medical assistance, many have their toes frozen off, other's feet are wounded by sharp ice or branches of trees lying on the snow. They suffer with inflammatory diseases of the throat and eyes.[9]

Campbell went on to suggest that the numerous dead horses lying around camp "in every direction" be removed before spring.[10]

The reports sent to Washington reveal the near-hopeless situation agents faced as refugees continued to stream into Kansas in a seemingly endless tide.[11] News of the starvation, malnutrition, exposure, and disease haunting the refugee camps spread via visitors who reported the deplorable conditions. Amputations of frozen limbs made the camps resemble a military hospital after a great battle, except many of these sufferers were young children. Agents in the field, moved by the misery they witnessed, acted beyond their authority and in some cases spent their own salaries to obtain supplies in the hope of warding off certain death for hundreds.[12] The Indian Office clearly could not handle the situation.

The United States government had to provide aid to these suffering people in the name of diplomacy if not humanity. Although the Lincoln administration had done little to keep the citizens of Indian Territory within the Union, the refugee situation offered a second chance to prove governmental goodwill. The natural choice to extend such a policy was the bureaucracy entrusted with the oversight of indigenous people. The Office of Indian Affairs (OIA) was ill-prepared to care for the influx of refugees, however, so the United States military stepped in as an emergency measure. Although initially welcomed, the intrusion of the military into the affairs of Indians created tension between the army and the OIA that continued throughout the war.[13]

The army maintained an organized presence in its Kansas forts prior to the OIA. Army garrisons and supplies enabled it to handle the initial tide of fleeing Indians far better than the Indian agents. William Coffin, chief of the Southern Superintendency, realized this immediately and appealed for assistance from Major General David Hunter, Department of Kansas. Hunter soon issued rations from military stores. The new food supply was vital for survival but could alleviate only the worst malnutrition in the refugee camps. Even this meager assistance proved short-lived, however, as Hunter backed away from the responsibility of feeding the Indians in February 1862. Congratulating himself on his duty to humanity, he returned the burden of care to the OIA.[14] The survival of the "loyal" Indians in Kansas depended on the efficiency of the Indian Office as of February 15, scarcely a comforting thought for those involved.

Agents of the Southern Superintendency faced the monumental task of ensuring the survival of some eight thousand people who possessed no food, tools, clothes, or shelter, and suffered from malnourishment, exposure and contagious disease. Scattered over a two hundred mile strip along the Verdigris River, the refugee camps endured at least a 10 percent death rate for humans and a catastrophic loss of ponies in the winter of 1862.[15] The task of caring for these people had to be accomplished in temporary offices without adequate funds. Funding offered the greatest challenge to officials charged with helping the Indians. Drawing on the credit of his salary—and his clerk's—Coffin worked toward a goal of supplying each person with shoes, socks, and a blanket, but admitted he could not achieve this for even half the population.[16] The ten thousand dollars worth of supplies he bought did not go far toward alleviating suffering. The Southern Superintendency's expenses totaled more than $98,500 for three months work with refugee Indians.[17]

In February 1862, Commissioner of Indian Affairs William Dole appointed Dr. William Kile as purchasing agent for the refugees. The Indian Office had no funds, and Dole's instructions to Kile candidly conceded that the greatest difficulty would be purchasing supplies solely on faith in the credit of the United States government. Everyone hoped for a congressional appropriation. The Secretary of the Interior wired his approval for buying on credit with such expectations, but funding from a Congress preoccupied with war in the East was far from guaranteed.[18] Despite these obstacles, the Southern Superintendency was determined to fulfill its responsibility more efficiently than the War Department. Coffin boasted that he could save 30 percent over the army's efforts by supporting the refugees on fifteen cents a day. To achieve this goal, the Indians would have to forego both coffee and sugar in their diet of cornmeal (cheaper and more readily available than flour) and beef, on or off the hoof. Although Coffin's plan provided basic sustenance, medical attention, clothing, cooking utensils, and tools remained in short supply.[19]

Transportation posed a major obstacle to the efficient delivery of goods. The location of camps on the Verdigris River protected the refugees from interaction with white residents but also required long transportation lines. Compounding the situation were the appalling sanitary conditions in existing camps resulting from thousands of decaying, starved horse carcasses. These factors prompted Coffin to remove all the refugees to the bottomlands of the Neosho River near LeRoy, Kansas. There the Indians encroached on white land, opening the possibility of conflict, but resided nearer to supply bases than their previous location.[20] Although this move improved the supply of food and clothing, shelter continued to be scarce. Visitors to the camps found crude shelters crafted from sticks and scraps of material so small "they were scarcely sufficient to cover the emaciated and dying forms beneath them." Agents regarded tents condemned for use by the army as a major improvement for their camps.[21] Tribal leaders did their best to help their people. Early in 1863 John Ross ordered Lewis Ross, the Cherokee Nation's treasurer, to purchase blankets, shoes, and other supplies to distribute among Cherokee refugees. The situation remained desperate, however.

No one involved in the refugee situation wanted it to continue—except perhaps white traders who sold inferior supplies to the Indian Office at inflated prices. Eager to be rid of the refugees, Commissioner Dole recommended purchasing only enough supplies for a thirty-day period. Refugees certainly shared his sentiments. Separated from families and wracked by malnutrition, exposure, and disease, they steadfastly resisted efforts to move them farther from their nations and sought only one remedy to their situation—returning home.[22] Everyone stressed the importance of timing and security in a successful relocation. It would do no good to move the people in the fall because they surely would starve over the winter. A short window of opportunity existed for a mass movement to Indian Territory. It had to be early enough in the spring to allow time for a crop to be planted but late enough to have grass for grazing. The requirement for safety proved even more difficult to achieve. Agents reiterated that the area had to be secured before the civilians arrived. The OIA operated with only a handful of inexperienced agents in temporary offices and lacked the resources to move refugees. If the refugees were to return home, it would be under the auspices of the United States Army.[23]

The Union failure to regain control of northern Indian Territory until late in the war had serious ramifications for displaced Cherokees. Initially, all hopes were pinned on the expedition of 1862. But when Salomon pulled the white troops out of the nation, essentially ceding control to the Confederates, the refugees found their hopes dashed. They would remain away from their homeland until the army tried again to regain control of the region in 1863. The U.S. Army buoyed the hopes of the refugees, informing them they would be protected in their homes in the spring of 1863. This was just the news they had been seeking, and many families moved back to the Cherokee Nation, fanning out across the country in their normal pattern of displaced settlement. This made them easy targets for the bushwhackers who roamed the region unchecked by a weak Union presence. Agents reported that the entire area was short on breadstuffs and that most of the cattle had been run out of the nation. The homecoming had been a mistake, and now 5,500–6,500 Cherokees were destitute.[24] Reports from the field remained gloomy. An agent borrowed flour from the army to feed the Cherokees, and prospects looked grim.

As the summer of 1863 wore on, circumstances barely improved. Most refugees remained clustered at Fort Gibson, the only place that afforded protection. By all accounts conditions were terrible. Supplies were expensive, hard to obtain, and even more difficult to transport. The Indian Office often spent up to a quarter of the funds for subsisting refugees on merely transporting the goods to the people. The Union Army only controlled about one and a half square miles, but had to support three thousand soldiers and six thousand refugees. Cherokee agent James Harlan set up headquarters in a barn, complained about the lack of army support, and reported the refugees as half-starved, naked, and sick.[25] It seemed to the Indian agents that their every attempt to help the refugees was thwarted by the army. Agents could not secure escorts to protect supply trains or military details to clear rebels from the area. They watched with frustration as Stand Watie's rebels burned the area around Park Hill and Tahlequah, passing within five miles of Fort Gibson without a Union response.[26] The army was not pleased with the situation either, and asked the OIA to return 1,200 refugees to Kansas, the last thing the Cherokees wanted.

The war had been a disaster for the loyal Cherokees. Their agent described their decline from being the most powerful, wealthy and intelligent Indians in the United States to utter destitution: "disgraced, humbled, impoverished, and demoralized." By November 1863, the government listed ten thousand loyal Cherokees on its rolls. Those officials who worked with the Cherokees recognized the bitter divisions between factions and predicted that rift would never be healed.[27] Conditions improved little in 1864. Agents continued to fret over the high costs of supplies, continued cattle theft, lack of transportation, and general suffering. The situation continued throughout the course of the war. It took years for all the refugees to make their way back because of poverty and continuing tensions between factions. Of course, many men who left as soldiers would never return.[28]

SOUTHERN SYMPATHIZERS

While loyal Cherokees suffered as refugees in Kansas, Missouri, and in their own nation, their Confederate brethren were also displaced. Just as the tide of the Union war effort was turning in 1863, so too did the balance of power shift in the Cherokee Nation. Union forces reestablished a measure of control in Indian Territory in 1863 with bases at Fort Gibson, Cherokee Nation, and Fort Smith, Arkansas. The return of refugees perhaps posed a greater threat to pro-Confederate citizens than even the Union army. Hundreds of loyal Cherokees returned to their nation with the Federal army. Their attempts to rebuild disrupted lives threatened the Confederate supporters who had remained in the nation during the great exodus of 1861 and 1862. Former refugees were now in a position to inflict retribution upon Confederate sympathizers, whom they believed had caused the loyal families' flight to Kansas and prolonged their refugee status. While some Cherokees rejoiced at the opportunity to return home in 1863, others fled in terror. Limited southward migrations in 1862 had been undertaken at a more reasonable pace, with time to pack and plan the journey. The panicked flight sparked by the arrival of Phillips's Federal troops saw rich and poor alike leave homes behind for an unknown life in exile.[29] Northern soldiers looting homes sometimes caught families in the midst of fleeing the turmoil. Soldiers took what they wanted, cleaning out smokehouses and breaking up wagons with impunity because no men remained to oppose them.

The new refugees moved south, away from Union territory and into the Choctaw and Chickasaw Nations and Texas. The Choctaws and Chickasaws supported the Confederacy from the beginning of the war, yet were scarcely touched by fighting or raiding. They passed the first half of the conflict relatively secure in their homes. But in 1863, thousands of refugees and the Confederate Indian forces descended on the hitherto untouched nations. The sudden influx of so many people placed great demands on the resources of the nations. The army needed food for the soldiers stationed at Scullyville, Choctaw Nation. Homeless refugees had no land, tools, or seed to grow their own crops and were forced to rely on what they could buy or borrow. These new circumstances taxed the resources of the host tribes beyond their limits. The Choctaw government had to supply provisions for needy families in the nation. The Choctaw council appropriated funds for the purchase of cotton and wool cards and food supplies. The food supply became so critical that Chief Peter Pitchlynn claimed corn for the sole use of Choctaw soldiers, in effect cutting off non-Choctaw Confederate forces. The situation deteriorated as lawlessness born of desperation and opportunity plagued the land. Pitchlynn issued a plea for restraint and good order and warned of penalties for transgressors.[30]

The flight of southern refugees differed from that of Opothleyahola's followers in 1861. The Confederate Indians traveled
south in small family or neighbor groups rather than on an
organized trek under a few leaders. No government agencies
awaited their arrival, and no provisions existed to feed, clothe,
or shelter them.[31] Most sought assistance from family and friends
or survived on their own. A lack of transportation posed a huge
problem. Wagons, carts, and draft animals remained in short
supply throughout the war. Those with money, such as the
William Penn Boudinot family, hired ferries to travel down river,
and then used ox teams to move overland. But most people
lacked such resources. Ingenuity could save the day as people
made sleds of poles to transport their few belongings. Foot
travel was the last choice for the long journey. Betsy Christie's
mother and aunts walked over one hundred miles to reach
safety at Doaksville, Choctaw Nation, where they congregated
with other women for protection.[32]

The gender composition of southern refugees was skewed,
even more so than the early Kansas refugee camps. Most pro-
Confederate Indian men had joined Stand Watie in 1863. Their
mothers, wives, sisters, and daughters often had to make the
long trek south alone. Some men took furloughs to escort their
families to safety. For example, William Cordray moved his
Cherokee family to Big Blue Creek in the Choctaw Nation, then
rejoined Stand Watie in the Cherokee Nation. Seeking safety in
numbers, people attempted to travel in groups of extended
family or friends. Many traveling groups remained together
while in exile, finding comfort in familiar faces. The relocation
of civilians meant long separations for husbands and wives,
however. Normal relations were suspended during the war years.
Numerous children born as refugees knew neither a sense of
home nor male authority. Although some men remained near
the refugee area and helped females obtain food, husbands
and fathers could not be with their families for long periods.

Alvin Hodge, a Creek Confederate soldier, provided food for a Cherokee girl named Mary Burgess, whom he later married.

Procuring food constituted the most important task of Indian refugees. Meat could be obtained in the form of wild game, still relatively abundant in the territory. As everywhere in Indian Territory, breadstuffs remained scarce throughout the war. Many families managed to grow a small crop despite their relocation.[33] The basic challenges of refugee life did not differ significantly between North and South. The demand for sustenance, safety, and shelter dominated survival efforts. In the Choctaw and Chickasaw Nations, as in Kansas, housing was at a premium. Returning soldiers attempted to build a crude log cabin to shelter women and children in their absence. Few families had tents, and some lived in houses made of mud and straw or cottonwood bark. Temporary shelters and often inadequate nutrition and water supplies raised the civilian death count. Large groups of refugees already suffering from want also faced the scourge of disease. Smallpox swept through refugee groups, as through military camps, with deadly results. The loss of valued relatives in a time of stress could be particularly difficult for refugee families. Any reduction in the number of people able to acquire food might mean hardship for several family members.[34]

Living as a refugee often meant going without accustomed services. Indians removed from larger towns such as Tahlequah or North Fork Town found themselves in much more isolated areas during the war. Families had to be more self-sufficient without towns or trading posts nearby. This situation fostered a sense of community among refugees, including those of different tribes and those who had been strangers. Communal activities such as hunting and dividing the kills enabled more people to withstand the demands of refugee life. It also reinforced more traditional patterns of Native life. A familiarity of culture that Cherokees found in the Choctaw and Chickasaw Nations may have provided some comfort to these displaced people. The relationship among members of the allied nations appears to have remained essentially positive. Certain refugees spoke highly of their Choctaw and Chickasaw neighbors. In some cases, Choctaw families aided the survival of temporary refugees. The influx of thousands of homeless individuals taxed the resources and patience of their hosts. By 1864, southern Indian Territory felt the pressure of the relocated population. Peter Pitchlynn described conditions as an unprecedented state of destitution and suffering. Still, the Choctaw and Chickasaw citizens did their best to support their displaced brethren from northern Indian Territory.[35]

The most fortunate refugee families had friends or relatives among the Choctaws and Chickasaws on whom they could rely for assistance. Mary Mackey Wilson came from a prominent Cherokee family. The Mackeys owned an important saltworks on the Illinois River and had extensive landholdings in the nation. Her father served as a captain in the Confederate commissary department. The women and children of the extended family, living at Fort Gibson and Webbers Falls, loaded into covered wagons and carriages, taking many of their possessions. Wealthy yet now homeless, the Mackey women traveled to the Blue River along with countless other displaced families. There they resided in their own cabin on the property of Jonathan Nail, a Choctaw who had a mill, store, and fine home. Despite the more comfortable surroundings, Mrs. Mackey died of pneumonia, leaving her children to the care of others.[36]

Wealth and status may have softened the hardships of refugee life, but it did not exempt the nation's elite from experiencing displacement. Indeed, it may have been more difficult to abandon expensive homes filled with fine furnishings than the simple log cabins of the majority of residents. Consider the influential Adair family. George Washington Adair signed the removal treaty and served as Watie's quartermaster until his

death; his son, Colonel William Penn Adair, was one of Stand
Watie's trusted officers. The Adairs, staunch Southern Cherokees,
would not be comfortable in the nation once Ross's adherents
dominated. Fear of attack by political rivals certainly was not new
to the family. The Adairs lived in a large house, easily defended
by thick walls and small windows, and slept with doors barred
and guards posted. The women and children left this home to
join the flood of refugees leaving the Cherokee Nation during
the war. They rolled their precious oil paintings onto broomstick
handles and left them with friends in Arkansas in an attempt to
protect their valuables. Despite careful preparations, the Adairs
lost almost everything on their journey to safety.[37]

REFUGEES TO TEXAS

Refugees who did not find temporary homes in the Choctaw
and Chickasaw Nations crossed the Red River into Texas.
Members of the most prominent families, including the Adairs,
Bells, and Waties, sat out the war in northern Texas. Stand
Watie's wife, Sarah, may have been the most famous Indian
refugee. Like Mrs. Robert E. Lee, Mrs. Stand Watie spent much
of the war in exile from her home, seeing little of her husband
or son who traveled constantly with the Confederate troops.
Obviously, Sarah could not remain unprotected in the Cherokee
Nation after Union activity rendered the area unsafe for Confederate sympathizers. Stand Watie's family would have made a
desirable target for Pins and Anti-Treaty party adherents. Sarah
Watie admitted that it was impossible for her to stay at home
and packed up her youngest children to move to Rusk County,
Texas, in May 1863. Nancy Bell Starr, Sarah's sister, had moved
to Rusk County along with several Cherokee families as early as
1854. There they built homes and established themselves for
half a decade before war split the Cherokee Nation. Families

found these relocated relatives a convenient haven from the upheavals at home.[38]

Sarah Watie had a dual motivation for moving her family. Northern Texas offered safety and better provisions than Indian Territory, and Sara's sister was extremely ill. Cherokees were a matrilineal people and the strong ties that bound female relatives brought Sarah to Nancy's side. In a more traditional era they might have shared a husband in the custom of polygamy, and although they did not follow this practice, Sarah and Nancy remained concerned about each other's family.[39]

Sarah did not go blindly into an unknown area, as many families did. She had visited Texas twice. This prior knowledge did nothing to ease the considerable rigors of the trip, however. James Bell urged travelers to have a good carriage and harness and fat, well-shod horses as early as 1854. They were encouraged to take clothing in sacks instead of trunks to reduce weight and also to carry horseshoe nails and a hammer, for the road was terrible.[40] If the journey to Texas had been considered arduous even with such advance preparation, its difficulty during wartime—when few modes of transportation remained and lawlessness prevailed—was daunting. Sarah Watie wrote to her husband frequently from Texas. She and Stand attempted to keep each other aware of their experiences through their long wartime separation. Their correspondence provides insight into the life of Texas refugees. Mrs. Stand Watie entered refugee life with a certain level of wealth and status and did not fear starvation or a lack of shelter, so the view she offered was that of more prosperous families.[41] The rigors of refugee life posed even greater challenges to less wealthy households, however, and many poorer families could not make the journey to Texas.

Female refugees devoted much of their energy to the welfare of absent family members. As a mother and wife, Sarah Watie naturally worried about the safety of her family. She frequently expressed concern for the well-being of her husband and eldest son Saladin, then serving under his father. Sarah had good reason to be concerned about their comfort and nourishment. Even the commander of the Confederate Cherokees often went without basic necessities of food and clothing. Sarah Watie and other refugee women attempted to supply relatives in the army by sending them clothing. By 1863 they could not buy clothing or cloth nor even obtain the supplies necessary to make cloth. Residents of both Indian Territory and its border regions begged for wool cards by the middle of the war. A scarce commodity, the cards commanded up to $105 per pair if they could be found at all. Women often were forced to distribute available resources between parts of their family. The Watie family had to share horses, obtained at a premium during the war, between a mounted military officer and a mother needing to travel for supplies.[42]

Moral conduct was as great a concern to mothers and wives as physical well-being.[43] Sarah urged Stand Watie to "be a good man as always" and maintain a clear conscience before God and man. Her admonition shows that the conditions of war did not destroy moral sensibilities. Individuals realized that hostilities would not last forever. Participants would return home and have to deal with the consequences of their actions. Mrs. Watie particularly worried about the effect of wartime conduct on the young men in the armies. News that her son and nephew had killed a prisoner produced a flurry of concern. "[I]t almost runs me crazy to hear such things," she wrote to Stand. The concerned mother instructed her husband "to tell my boys to always show mercy as they expect to find God merciful to them." She worried that because of this early exposure to condoned killing, Saladin would never value human life as he should. A mother's empathy extended even to the enemy. Sarah gave Stand specific instructions not to kill William Ross if he were caught, but instead to hold him for the duration of the war. She admitted that "they all deserve death," but she had empathy for Ross's old mother. Education also concerned mothers. Sarah Watie's letters are filled with references to her struggle to keep the youngest children in school. The availability of schooling influenced where she lived, and even prompted the separation of the remaining family unit. Despite, or perhaps because of, the disruption of family life caused by the war, women such as Sarah Watie attempted to provide some continuation of their previous lifestyle.[44]

Women tried to recreate a home for their children while in exile, but some intangible features could never be duplicated. A constant sense of discomfort from living outside known, comfortable community circles prevailed. Historian Mary Elizabeth Massey notes that white southern refugee women also experienced a sense of displacement as uninvited outsiders in someone else's neighborhood. The abrupt change from living in closely knit communities within their own nations to that of a nomadic life moving among larger white towns must have caused considerable anxiety for Indian refugees. In addition, relations with new neighbors were not always cordial. Refugees attempted to appreciate the safety offered by their newly adopted communities, but rancor still existed. Although Sarah Watie endeavored to keep petty problems and complaints from entering her correspondence to her husband, she occasionally inserted comments about neighbors and wondered at the "experiences of these white folks." She bristled at criticism of her husband's actions as a leader and her sense that people in Texas did not wholeheartedly support the cause for which Stand Watie fought. The apparent lack of commitment to the cause from people who had not experienced the horrors of war especially galled Mrs. Watie. She believed the residents of Texas had not experienced war as Cherokees had and thought they "ought all to feel the effects of this war so that they would know to feel for the soldiers."[45]

Saladin Ridge Watie served in the Confederate Cherokee forces
under his father. Courtesy of the Oklahoma Historical Society.

Another point of contention between refugees and Texas
residents concerned the purchasing of supplies. Sarah Watie
complained of speculation and price gouging that seemed
to take unfair advantage of displaced Indians in contracted

circumstances. Her disgust at such activity reflected sensibilities she shared with her husband. Reporting news of army officers involved in speculation, Sarah admonished her husband to stay clear of such schemes. She felt so strongly about the matter that she vowed to live on bread and water rather than have it said that Stand speculated off his people. The idea of leaders exploiting their dependents rather than redistributing goods for their support ran counter to traditional Native values. Indeed, the principle of reciprocity to kin and neighbors that aided refugees within the Indian nations was scarce in the states. For their part, Texans did not view the flood of impoverished and desperate women and children with any kind of favor. These newcomers brought little money to inject into a war torn economy. In fact, they were likely to require assistance from Texans in order to survive. The disfavor with which Texans regarded refugees can be seen in the head tax placed on Indian exiles south of the Red River.[46]

Conditions did not improve for refugees displaced from their homes. Shortages grew worse, tempers shorter, and the welcome mat more worn. Neither refugees nor their reluctant hosts desired that the situation continue even one more month. The tide of refugees streaming south peaked in 1863, but for as long as troops rode through the Indian nations it did not entirely abate. Thousands of Cherokees were living outside the borders of their nation when Stand Watie finally surrendered in the summer of 1865. Perhaps most indicative of the effect of the Civil War on the Five Nations, hundreds remained away from their homes in 1866 and 1867.[47]

WOMEN AND AFRICAN AMERICANS

Two groups generally referred to as minorities came into a different status due to wartime conditions in the Cherokee Nation—women and blacks. Mothers, sisters, daughters, underage sons, and slaves filled the refugee camps and homesteads. As discussed previously, it was often not practical for able-bodied men to remain at home, and few did. This left a skewed gender and race population to deal with the harsh realities of civilian wartime life. The same condition existed in many areas in the country, most similarly in southern regions where women and slaves coexisted on the homefront.[48] Parallels between the experiences of white women and Indian women coping with wartime conditions obviously existed; some aspects of gender and power were remarkably constant. Native culture added another facet to the situation in the Cherokee Nation, however.

The degree to which the experience of Cherokee women differed from that of most white women depended on the extent of their movement toward Euro-American norms. Traditional Cherokee culture was matrilineal and matrilocal, resulting in a powerful female role in society. Women owned homes, controlled lineages, conveyed clan membership, and wielded some political power. As the producers of life and subsistence they held an integral role in Cherokee society. On a practical level, women were the Cherokee farmers, and thus could till, sow, harvest, churn butter, and feed their families. For women still operating in a traditional pattern, the wartime loss of manpower might not be that disruptive to their normal patterns. They could continue their roles as agriculturalists, while fathers and husbands took up their responsibilities as warriors. Wartime shortages would certainly make this harder, but it would not be psychologically distressing nor require new skills. Such traditional women may well have been the majority of Cherokee women in the 1860s.[49] Unfortunately, we have scant historical evidence of their lives. Probably illiterate, they did not leave journals, diaries, or letters as records of their experience.

The women most likely to have recorded their wartime travails were those who had slipped into the Euro-American pattern of male dominated agriculture and thus struggled with a new occupation during the conflict. Cherokee women who moved away from traditional matrilineal control of crops now faced a new reality more similar to white women in other areas of the South. In better circumstances a return to the earlier system of agriculture which empowered women through their control of and contribution to a major part of the family's food supply might have been welcome, but in time of war and constant deprivation it was only an added burden. Like women across the country who had been abandoned by their protectors and providers, acculturated Cherokee women wrestled with problems of taking on new responsibilities. Providing for a family was never easy, but in wartime Indian Territory it could be almost impossible. Whether at home in an altered landscape or far away in a refugee situation, achieving the basic necessities of life became an ordeal for women unaccustomed to the activity. The trials of wartime drove many women to seek an end to the strife. Just as historian Drew Gilpin Faust found to be the case among white Confederate women, Cherokee women often begged their husbands to come home from the war so they could resume normal patterns.[50] Even the wife of the Confederate Cherokee's beloved commander was thoroughly sick of the hardships of war by 1864. Sarah Watie longed for peace to "feel no dread of war."[51]

Wealthy slaveholding Cherokee women had to make the same adjustments as their white counterparts in the South. Slaves performed many of the basic tasks of farming, running a household, and raising children. The uncertainties of war—refugee status, violence, and economic hardship—meant that slaves were often no longer available for such work, and it all fell on the shoulders of Cherokee mistresses. Status as elite women did not prepare them for the difficulties of farming, household labor, managing slaves, or lending support to army.

Overall, Cherokee women experienced the war differently depending on their previous lifestyles. Adherence to traditional Cherokee gender roles might have made the loss of male assistance less onerous. Traditional roles, on the other hand, might not have offered much comfort in terms of safety in a lawless land, nor substantially altered the reality of chronic shortages of subsistence materials. Women who had moved toward a Euro-American, particularly southern, pattern of separate and unequal gender spheres certainly had to make more adjustments when left on their own during the war. Many of those women would have had greater access to wealth and power, which in turn might have eased their burdens somewhat. For many southern women slaveholding was a mixed blessing in wartime, providing labor but also constant concern over the protection of slave "property." Cherokee women's war experience both mirrored that of non-Native women and also added a new dimension because of matrilineal cultural traditions.

One large group of people in Indian Territory did not fit conveniently into categories of rebel or loyal, Cherokee or Creek, civilian or soldier. As a legacy of over two hundred years of contact with Europeans, southeastern Native groups included an often overlooked diversity. Thousands of African Americans lived in the nations and shared the fate of their Native neighbors.[52] This minority group within a minority nation defies easy categorization. Some lived free, although not equal, while others were held in bondage by Cherokee owners. In almost every case, such individuals had even less power than their Native American neighbors when the war came.

To an even greater degree than Indian residents, black families in Indian Territory found themselves suddenly caught in the turmoil of warfare. Largely unable to participate in national decision making, black slaves and freedpeople still retained a measure of control over their future. Slaves throughout the

American South were denied the opportunities of literacy, political standing, or public voice, yet they knew about the division between North and South. Some understood the changes war could bring, and many were poised to take advantage of new situations to obtain freedom.[53]

Slave experience in the Cherokee Nation varied widely, partly because not all slaveholders sided with the Confederacy. Those who did tended to relocate. Many who moved south to Texas or to the Choctaw Nation attempted to take slaves with them. The circumstances of hasty flight allowed for the possibility of escape or separation from slaveholders. Additionally, the lifestyle of refugees generally was not conducive to retaining control over slaves. Unexpected journeys and uncertain living arrangements characterized refugee life. John Harrison and his mother traveled with their owner from the Creek Nation to Fort Washita, then to Texas, and finally returned to Indian Territory. Such mobility undermined traditional measures of behavioral control.[54]

Some slaves held by Indians seized the wartime opportunity to improve their situation. As in the rest of Confederate territory, Union lines—in this case Kansas—proved a strong lure for those daring enough to attempt escape. Young, healthy, single men had the best chance of surviving the sometimes harrowing trek to a Federal camp. It seemed to slaveholders that all who could survive the journey tried it: "[T]he few [slaves] who have not gone over to the Federals," remarked one owner, "are either old, infirm, or sick."[55] Unhindered by the burden of small children, male slaves benefited from greater mobility than females. In many cases they already enjoyed travel privileges in order to visit families on other farms. Operating as individuals, they were better able to take advantage of opportunities for freedom.[56]

Although individuals naturally benefited from successful escapes, flight from bondage could have repercussions on those left behind. Security might be tightened or punishments meted out. Often the loss of one person's labor meant the remaining slaves were forced to pick up the slack. Mary Stinnett found herself in this position while living in Texas with her owner. Her husband, George, took off for the North and the freedom promised by Union territory, leaving Mary to perform his field work in addition to her own tasks in the house. In addition to cooking, cleaning, serving, and mending, Mary added breaking ground with an ox team.[57] Slave women could also pay a high price for the loss of male protectors. When the men in her world—owner and father—left for the war, Victoria Thompson was stolen by a white man who forced her to live with him and also branded her.

Male slaves also experienced mobility by going to war as personal servants. They accompanied Indian slaveholders into the army just as many slaves from Virginia or South Carolina did. Evidence suggests that the chance to escape a boring routine or the opportunity to see the world may have motivated those who went to war.[58] A Cherokee family, the Taylors, traded some land for a slave named Doc Hayes. The eight members of his extended family were the only slaves on the Taylors' small farm in the Flint District. When the war broke out, Mr. Taylor left home to fight with Stand Watie, and Doc Hayes accompanied him. They left behind to survive as best they could Indian and black women. Because of their Confederate sympathies, the women of the Taylor household were harassed by Pin Indians and lost sheep, feather beds, and horses to the pro-Union raiders. Mrs. Taylor finally fled to Texas with her slaves, leaving her property to be destroyed.[59]

The majority of slaves remained at home. Some owners expected slaves to care for their families while they went off to fight, while others commanded servants to guard their property when the family sought safety. The effectiveness of the latter was dubious, although former slave Ed Butler insisted that he would never abandon this responsibility until his owner returned.[60] Being left on one's own in an area bereft of the normal strictures of society might have seemed like a boon to slaves; the reality was often harsh, however. As Indian Territory suffered from a lack of food and transportation and a surplus of violence, slaves generally had difficulty acquiring the resources necessary for survival. What few supplies households retained could be taken in one raid. Elsie Gardner remembered being entrusted with the responsibility of guarding her owner's clothes. Each time she heard soldiers coming, she carried the clothes out into the swamp to hide. One time while she engaged in this exercise, two hundred soldiers raided the smokehouse, fed their horses in the corn crib, killed the turkeys, and stole cooking utensils.[61]

Life changed for many of those who remained in bondage. Slaveholders realized that the value of their chattel hung in the balance of the war. Sarah Watie expected that she would have to sell her "boys" if the tide changed in Texas. Some owners were reluctant to continue supporting an investment that they might soon lose. Jim Threat's owner thus decided to execute old slaves during the war as resources grew scarce. Even when abuse was not that blatant, slaves were the first to suffer when food and clothes were in short supply. Additionally, slaveholders could be expected to attempt to tighten control over their property during tumultuous times.[62] Fear induced them to initiate new restrictions including less travel, more work, heightened discipline, and possibly greater violence. Privileges such as visiting family members might be curtailed in an effort to prevent slaves from running away. Furthermore, owners might try to obtain maximum work from a resource they could soon lose. As one eyewitness remembered, "Everybody was harder on their slaves then."[63]

The Union Army, rather than owners, became the most disruptive force in the lives of Indian-owned slaves. Historians have characterized the Federal Army west of the Mississippi River as an army of emancipation. Wherever Federal forces marched they encouraged slaves to seize their freedom. The arrival of the Union Army in Park Hill, Cherokee Nation, prompted a general uprising among slaves who asserted their freedom by helping themselves to horses and weapons and joining a "swelling throng on its way to join the Federal army." Liberation could also involve force, resulting in soldiers chasing slaves from the only home they had to an uncertain future. Lonian Moses belonged to Lewis Ross, one of the largest slaveholders in the Cherokee Nation, owning 150 persons. When Union troops came through the nation in 1862 they declared the slaves free. Still, many slaves did not want to leave because they feared retribution. Many slaves saw the Union presence as a fleeting one and feared a lack of protection in their new status as freedmen.[64]

Federal soldiers seemed more interested in punishing slave-holders than aiding slaves. Despite their misgivings, Ross's slaves had to load the master's finest possessions onto wagons. All the draft animals were pressed into service and all available livestock driven off. Reveling in their roles as liberators and profiting from the looting of wealthy enemies, Union men failed to grasp the situation from the slaves' point of view. They never considered what it would mean to the slaves if Confederates caught them with fine furnishings and other costly items. When they left the slave train at the Kansas border, the thoughtless soldiers only added to the fears of those they had liberated by warning them not to be taken by the Indians. The group of Cherokee slaves, fearful of the reprisals should they be found with Indian men's riches, immediately broke the fine furnishings and turned loose the livestock.[65]

The Cherokee freedpeople often found relocation to be a mixed blessing. Those who reached Kansas were harassed by bushwhackers, unable to accumulate property, and barely able to survive even through much hard work. Thousands of Cherokee and Creek slaves came to Fort Gibson, Cherokee Nation, either sent by Federal troops or seeking refuge on their own. The relief from reaching a safe haven amid the turmoil of war was probably short-lived. Soldiers at the fort could barely defend themselves and their supplies from Confederate raids, much less care for contraband. Some black families found themselves in worse conditions than they had experienced at their owners' homes.[66]

One means of survival in the poverty-plagued area around Fort Gibson could be found in making a military connection. The Tomm family pursued this course. Their owner took the father, a blacksmith, to Texas to care for the white family. Left behind, the mother and her young son Jim hid in the cellar at home until discovered by soldiers. Conveyed in wagons to Fort Gibson, they were reunited with Jim's older brother who had gone north with loyal Creeks to enlist with the Indian Home Guards. This family connection to the United States Army enabled Jim and his mother to get enough to eat while refugees at the fort. Many other families were not so lucky. Rochelle Ward remembered black people camped everywhere around Fort Gibson. Hundreds of people crowded within a half mile of the fort, afraid to venture far from the protection of soldiers' guns. There they struggled for subsistence while listening in terror to nearby skirmishes. Decimated by outbreaks of disease such as cholera, slaves in refugee camps waited out the war and the arrival of emancipation.[67]

Indian-owned slaves faced the same cruel dilemma as other slaves throughout the South. When the news of freedom finally arrived, emancipated blacks found themselves without food, shelter, or clothing, and little means to acquire them. Children remembered family predicaments. "Father was stumped for he didn't know what on earth he was going to do with that big family," recalled one witness. "We had no home, no food and mighty few clothes." Some enterprising women turned the skill they had been taught, cooking for their owners, into a means for survival. Others wrested a bare living from the land as they drifted about and attempted to establish homes for their families. In some ways, emancipation was as difficult as slavery, and it took many years for freedmen to achieve a level of security.[68]

The Civil War brought immense suffering to Indian Territory. White, black, or Indian, few families remained untouched by the upheavals and horrors of war. The Cherokees had joined the dominant white governments in their war only to experience a brutal baptism by fire. Conditions for civilians varied from place to place and from time to time, yet the constantly shifting military front spread the trauma throughout the region. Many who were secure early in the war fled their homes in later years. Plagued by shortages of food, clothing, and shelter, terrorized by random violence, and forced into new social and economic roles, civilian residents may have had an even more horrific war experience than Indian soldiers. The Cherokee Nation endured widespread disruption and destruction. Violence, shortages, and endless uncertainty and tension combined to take a heavy toll. The social, political, and economic losses endured by Cherokee society persisted long after the war.[69]

Epilogue

They need food, clothing, tools, everything in fact, to begin life again.

D. N. COOLEY

The Civil War ended in 1865, but the consequences for residents of Indian Territory lasted for decades. The postwar period in the South is a familiar tale of adjustment to an altered social, political, and economic order. The Cherokees endured an equivalent time of upheaval within their nation. All members of the nation—elite and poor, traditional and progressive—faced a changed world, but the elite arguably lost more primarily because they had more to lose. Physical losses as well as the economic, social, and political upheaval of the war years were unprecedented. Somehow the Cherokees, again guided by their elite, had to find the means to rebuild.[1]

The establishment of peace followed four years of conflict that had left nothing untouched. Cherokee country had endured all forms of combat, from pitched battles to guerilla raids. The area around Fort Gibson witnessed the most frequent activity of opposing armies. Dozens of homes in the wealthy Park Hill neighborhood were reduced to ashes; only the Murrell house survived to symbolize past grandeur. Vast stretches of territory remained unpopulated because civilians had fled. Tens of thousands of Indian people died because of the war. A lack of census data for the critical years precludes a precise reckoning of loss, but some estimates put the death rate for Indian Territory at 50 percent. The OIA attempted a rough count of surviving Indians in the fall of 1865, noting 14,000 Cherokees. The Cherokee population apparently declined from 21,000 to 14,000 during the war period, a 33 percent loss. In addition to outright losses, countless widows and orphans created by the conflict underscored the disintegration of family life.[2]

Many communities suffered almost total destruction. Observers groped for words to describe the desolation they witnessed. Most farms had been abandoned. Fields were overgrown and fences missing. Only chimneys marked the spots where comfortable cabins once stood. The entire social fabric had disintegrated. Schools, churches, missions, and most businesses no longer operated. Religion, politics, education, and social life had been disrupted by the war. The process of rebuilding was in many ways similar to the reconstruction of Cherokee life required after removal. Foundations of social institutions existed after the Civil War, but the people had to find both the will and the means to reestablish all that they had lost.[3] Many were in a situation similar to that of Susan Campbell, begging from neighbors for the resources to start over. A friend recalled that "last spring her [Campbell] house was burnt and she lost all she possessed she came to this neighborhood in search of seed Corn—we let her have a bushel she went home broke up her ground, planted her corn, and raised a fine crop."[4]

Although much could be repaired, structures rebuilt, and farms replanted, some damage proved to be permanent. The disappearance of cattle as a result of widespread rustling ranked high among the most obvious long-term losses. Estimates place the number of cattle run out of Indian Territory into Kansas at 300,000 head, worth $4 million. The scope of the thievery was

Hunter's Home. George Murrell's home is the only antebellum Park Hill residence to survive today. Courtesy of the Library of Congress.

remarkable and involved accusations against OIA agents, touching on an oft-heard claim of corruption in the government bureaucracy overseeing Indian welfare. The army was involved as well, as evidenced by the assertion that "while our men are bravely battling for the Union cause, United States citizens and soldiers are stripping our country of cattle and horses. . . . This is done by contractors and officers of the United States army."[5] Fraud at the expense of Natives would continue to be a hallmark of the government, but the immediate consequence of the cattle raids for the Indians was the loss of a critical food supply and personal wealth that would never be recovered.[6] The combination of theft and destruction left many formerly prosperous Indian Territory residents impoverished and dependent on the government for survival. In October 1865, the government still subsisted 17,000 Indians.[7]

The end of hostilities in 1865 found citizens of all nations scattered both within and outside the territorial borders. Unionists held sway in the Cherokee Nation, and most southern sympathizers remained afraid to return to their homes. Bitter rivalries kept the displaced Confederate families in the Choctaw and Chickasaw Nations or across the Red River in Texas. The Cherokee people remained divided politically and geographically. The OIA southern superintendent feared that hatreds were so deep "no human power can reconcile" the Cherokee factions. He estimated that 10,500 Cherokees had been loyal to the Union, while 6,500 supported the South. Most of the loyal element returned to the Cherokee Nation by 1865, but the disloyal Cherokees remained refugees near the Red River. As 1865 drew to a close, thousands of Indians—including Stand Watie—lived away from their homes.[8]

Political aspects of the postwar period proved even more devastating to the welfare of the nations than the economic and social conditions. The end of the war brought the inevitable round of negotiations. Meetings held in 1865 intended not only to reestablish peace but also to restructure the position of the independent Native nations within the United States. Postwar treaty negotiations began the relatively brief journey from tribal autonomy to dissolution of the Native nations. The federal government entered this phase of diplomacy determined to wrest land from the Five Nations. Guilty or innocent, treasonous or loyal—these counted for less than the richness of unoccupied landholdings. The forces that Creek Chief George Washington Grayson referred to as "ruthless greed" acted as powerful enemies of Indian sovereignty.[9]

The 1866 treaty negotiations created an embarrassing record of greed, bullying, and lack of understanding of Indian culture on the part of the United States commissioners. From beginning to end, government negotiators sought to gain as much as possible from the Indians. Nations that had provided more than 3,500 soldiers for the Union cause, and endured an enormous percentage of military losses, did not expect to pay a high price for the privilege of maintaining relations with the federal government.[10] Yet Commissioner of Indian Affairs Dennis Cooley consistently demanded reparations. Lobbyists and speculators attended the treaty talks and successfully pressed their case through federal negotiators. Kansas hoped to expel its Native population to Indian Territory; the forfeiture of land for this purpose became part of the treaty. Railroad interests also demanded and won considerable rights for lines through Indian land.[11]

Federal commissioners met the representatives of the Five Nations at Fort Smith, Arkansas, in September 1865. The commission included Commissioner of Indian Affairs Dennis Cooley who presided and acted as spokesman, his Southern Superintendent, Elijah Sells, Brigadier General William Harney, called "the butcher" by Plains Indians, Colonel Ely S. Parker, probably thought to be relevant to the discussion because he was a Seneca Indian, and as a last minute addition, Quaker philanthropist Thomas Wister. This group traveled to Arkansas, as it turned out, not only to deal with the Indian Nations. They also met with lobbyists and politicians from Kansas who clamored for the opportunity to solve their "Indian problem" by relocating unwanted tribes to Indian Territory. This round of treaty making with supposedly defeated tribes was their golden opportunity. The council was unable to achieve anything more than the establishment of formal peace before the talks were moved to Washington in 1866. Those few weeks, however, sent an ominous message of the government's intention toward the Indian nations. The federal commissioners took the position that all of the Indian nations were traitors for joining the Confederacy and had forfeited their rights under previous treaties. New treaties must be written. Not surprisingly, these new treaties would include new conditions—primarily land cessions.

The Cherokees remained divided after the cessation of hostilities and thus sent two groups to the council. The Loyal Cherokee delegation—Lewis Downing, Smith Christie, and H. D. Reese—arrived at Fort Smith first and settled in to listen to Cooley. His opening remarks sounded innocuous enough. He claimed the United States was eager to resume relations with the Indians as they had existed before the war. It immediately became apparent, however, that the commission had no intention of returning to the status quo. As political and military appointees of a recently victorious government, they meant to leverage their perceived power to the utmost extent. All the Indian nations had to agree to several stipulations laid out by Cooley. Not unexpectedly, they would sign a treaty for permanent peace and abolish slavery. Unlike Confederate states, however, Indians were to incorporate freedmen into the nations on an equal basis. After that the requirements became increasingly demanding. The "civilized" Indians would now have to assist in forcing the "wild" Plains tribes to stop fighting each other and whites. Finally the activities of the lobbyists became clear when the commissioners demanded that the nations yield land for the settlement of soon to be removed Kansas tribes. Additionally, no white men except officials could live in the territory unless a tribe formally incorporated them. This provision might stem the flow of opportunistic whites onto Indian lands, but was also reminiscent of Georgia's trampling of Cherokee sovereignty which resulted in *Worcester v. Georgia.* It is a measure of sovereign nations that they control access to their own lands and do not accept the dictates of another power. The most shocking requirement of the commissioners insisted that the whole territory be consolidated under one government. Though unspoken, this was plainly a precursor to the eventual statehood of the region. Indeed, Senate bill 459, passed in August 1865, authorized the organization of Indian Territory. The attack on Indian sovereignty was clear.[12]

The worst was yet to come for the Cherokees. Cooley knew that his demands would engender strong opposition, especially among those who considered themselves allies of the United States. Indeed, the Cherokee delegation protested being treated as enemies; Cooley countered by bringing up the 1861 Cherokee treaty of alliance with the Confederacy. This piece of paper would only go so far, however, to control a group whose men had fought and died in the service of the United States Army. Loyal Cherokees might reasonably expect to be rewarded for their service and compensated for their losses by the federal government. Cooley needed to strengthen his hand and he did so by attacking the Cherokees' main strength—Chief John Ross. Everyone knew Ross to be a clever and persistent politician with formidable bargaining and leadership skills. The commissioners could not hope to gain all their demands, which included extensive Cherokee land holdings, with Ross leading the Cherokees. Thus Cooley set out to discredit the venerable chief. Branding Ross as a traitor, Cooley began a nasty campaign to refuse recognition of Ross's authority. This ran counter to the realization of Cooley's predecessor, William Dole, that Ross had entered a Confederate alliance out of expediency. Nevertheless, Cooley's annual report recorded assertions that Ross was "still at heart an enemy of the U.S." and "disposed to breed discord among his people."[13]

In reality, the discord among the Cherokees was fomented by the United States. The government took every advantage of the long history of division within the nation. The Southern Cherokee delegation arrived at Fort Smith, led by Stand Watie and Elias C. Boudinot, former Cherokee delegate to the Confederate Congress. This group proved much more amenable to negotiation with the United States than their northern counterparts. Boudinot "cheerfully" agreed with the commissioners' demands, with the predictable exception of equality for Cherokee freedmen and the call for a consolidated government. Not only did the Confederate Cherokees resist consolidation, they had no desire to unite with the Ross faction. Boudinot demanded that the Cherokee Nation be divided because, he said, the two adversarial factions could not be "expected to live in an undivided country." In a blatant gambit to be ingratiating, Boudinot also declared Cooley's plan to be "one of the grandest and noblest schemes ever devised for the red men."[14] The meetings ended with little accomplished but plenty of tension on all sides, leading to the unfortunate collapse of elderly Chief Ross.

Treaty talks resumed in Washington in January 1866. The relocation of the proceedings placed an enormous hardship on tribal representatives, forcing them to incur expensive bills for traveling and staying in the capital. This seemed especially wasteful at a time when their people faced starvation at home. It also deprived the nations of their strongest leaders in an extremely difficult period of adjustment after the war. The stage was set by the United States, however, and the Indian nations had to respond. Refusing to be passive victims, the Five Nations had representatives and legal counsel in Washington who acted on their behalf. The Choctaws and Chickasaws struck the best

The Cherokees remained divided at the end of the war. Former Confederates sent their own delegation to Washington. Courtesy of the Oklahoma Historical Society.

deal with the government, gaining a settlement deemed by scholars to be the "least reconstructive" of all the treaties.[15] The Creeks and Seminoles lost a great deal of land in their treaties but managed to reunite their societies after the divisions of the war.[16]

The Cherokees suffered the worst reconstruction experience. Much of their hardship arose from chronic factionalism. Commissioner Cooley knew what he wanted from the Indian nations and would use whatever means available. The Cherokees presented him with the opportunity to play one faction against the other to extract a deal favorable to the government. Cherokee negotiations in Washington mirrored the removal meetings of three decades before in that the nation sent two teams to argue its case. Chief John Ross, recovered but weak, headed one group; Stand Watie and Elias C. Boudinot opposed him.[17] The Southern or Treaty party, intent on obtaining a permanent division of the Cherokee Nation and by background favorable to white intervention it deemed progress, supported railroad right-of-ways, territorial government, and essentially anything that Cooley demanded. Jumping to take advantage of the compliance of the southern Cherokee faction, Cooley continued his effort to discredit Ross, whom he correctly viewed as the major obstacle to the government's plans for the Cherokee. Cooley published his charges in a pamphlet titled *The Cherokee Question*, forcing Ross, in the last days of his life, to endure scathing attacks on his character and leadership. The situation devolved into a hurtful, vindictive battle of pamphlets, with both sides purporting to state the Cherokee situation.

Treaty negotiations dragged through the first half of 1866, requiring the Cherokee delegates to endure a long stay in the federal capital while their families struggled thousands of miles away, some still refugees outside the nation. Stand Watie, perhaps more accustomed to actions than to endless meetings, returned to his family. Ross fought declining health from a hotel room. Despite his deteriorating condition, Ross remained a master politician and directed the Loyal Cherokees' efforts from behind the scenes.

The Unionist Cherokees attempted to circumvent the hostility of the Office of Indian Affairs by presenting memorials directly to Congress and President Andrew Johnson in which they proclaimed both their loyal war service and their objections to a consolidated government in the Territory. Of course, they also condemned their rivals in the Southern Cherokee delegation, a favor quickly returned by Watie and company in their own letters to the administration. The Cherokees must have looked like easy targets to government officials. The tribe's long-standing factionalism resulted in infighting more detrimental to the cause of sovereignty than any government policy. While fighting for their existence, the Cherokees continued to swipe and stab at each other.

John Ross proved to be a formidable adversary to both Cherokees and whites who tried to thwart his goals for the Cherokee Nation. Ross managed to meet directly with President Johnson to protest the poor treatment from Commissioner Cooley. Then he attempted to circumvent Cooley by dealing directly with his superior, Secretary of Interior Harlan. Proceeding as a strong ally of the United States, the Ross delegation presented a treaty predicated on the fact that all previous treaties between the parties were still in effect, pointedly repudiating Cooley's position that the Cherokees had forfeited their rights. While the loyalist Cherokees generously granted protection of rights and property to their southern brethren, they also asserted control over railroad land grants, criminal and civil jurisdiction in the nation, and the access of other tribes to the Cherokees' excess lands.[18] Meanwhile, the Southern delegation focused primarily on the division of land and money. Cooley naturally favored this plan and entered into a treaty with the former Confederate Cherokees. The Ridge-Boudinot group had stooped low to get their way, choosing to demonize fellow Cherokees in pursuit of political gains. John Rollin Ridge wrote a livid description of Northern Cherokees during the war cutting men to pieces with "demoniacal glee" and scalping Northern soldiers. This approach fed the worst white stereotypes about barbarous Natives and discredited all Indians.

Many observers would have judged the game to be over and the victory with the Southern Cherokees. The members of the Southern delegation certainly believed it had prevailed and sent word to Stand Watie to begin organizing a new government. When it declared that John Ross's "day is done," however, it spoke too soon.[19] The old chief refused to yield to a division of his Cherokee Nation and fought hard to counteract Cooley's decision by lobbying Congress and the President to refuse ratification. He worked behind the scenes with Radical Republicans predisposed to distrust Confederates and rallied public opinion to his side from the editorial pages of the *New York Tribune*. The treaty was rejected.

After the failure of this first treaty, Cooley and his boss, Secretary of Interior Harlan, came under pressure to settle the matter. Treaty negotiations with the Ross delegation resumed, yielding a treaty finally ratified by the Senate and proclaimed on August 11, 1866. The powerful Cherokee voice behind the settlement—John Ross—died on August 1, but not before he learned that the government had recognized both his loyalty and leadership of the Cherokee Nation. The final treaty conceded much but retained what Ross had fought for most of his life to achieve—a single western Cherokee Nation.[20] He knew that the greatest threat to continued Cherokee sovereignty was division. Instead, the Confederate Cherokees received only the Canadian district in which they could settle and select officials. They did receive amnesty for crimes relating to the recent war and an annulment of the wartime Cherokee confiscation laws. The stress and fury over the loss of their political goals brought out the worst in the Southern delegates when cousins Ridge

and Boudinot hurled accusations toward each other and dis-
avowed their kinship ties.[21] The treaty also enabled the sale of
the Cherokee Neutral Lands, settlement of the Kansas Indians
on unoccupied Cherokee lands, and specified a two hundred
foot right-of-way for railroads, considerably less than lobbyists
had expected.[22]

The reconstruction treaties left all Five Nations weaker and
less autonomous, driving a deep wedge into the armor of Native
sovereignty. No southern states were forced to surrender land
to the federal government, but it was a predetermined fact in
the negotiations with Indians. The Cherokee Nation gave up
territory so the government could pursue its goal of concen-
trating all unwanted Native people in Indian Territory. In a
requirement that both paralleled and exceeded demands made
on former Confederate slave owners, Indian slaves had to be
adopted into the tribes or given land with their new freedom.[23]
This action had important ramifications for the future racial
composition of Oklahoma, but its major effect was to strike a
severe blow against Indian national sovereignty. No longer
could the nations decide their own tribal membership or system
of land distribution. The government even forced them to
admit members of other tribes to citizenship. Moreover, non-
Indians, in the role of government agents, railroad interests,
cattlemen, and settlers, would continue to chip away at the
rights of the Five Nations. The final chapter of the Civil War in
Indian Territory foretold a future struggle for Native autonomy
that culminated in Oklahoma statehood.[24]

POSTWAR LIVES

In many ways, the history of a place or its people is a tale of
individual lives. Several of those prominent in the saga of the
Civil War in the Cherokee Nation endured still more hardship

Cherokee Capitol Building, Tahlequah. After the war, the Cherokees had to rebuild much of their infrastructure, including governmental buildings that had been burned by Watie's forces. The grounds include monuments to John Ross and Stand Watie. Courtesy of Western History Collections, University of Oklahoma.

following the end of hostilities. The nation was not reunited with all its refugee citizens home until 1867, and afterward it faced the monumental task of rebuilding lives shattered by war.

Chief John Ross was an old and tired man by the end of the war. He lost his dear wife Mary, his beautiful home, and much of the prosperity of his people. Although suffering from ill health, Ross labored to achieve the long-desired unity that had proved so elusive. The Cherokee Nation remained intact geographically but continued to be plagued by factionalism. John Ross died far from his beloved Cherokee Nation in Washington, D.C., on August 1, 1866.[25] At one time a man of substantial wealth, Ross died in debt, another fortune destroyed by the tides of war. William Ross, his nephew, was chosen to complete his uncle's term as chief.

Stand Watie officially ceased hostilities on June 25, 1865, in the Choctaw Nation, and was the last Confederate general to surrender. In Washington for treaty negotiations, Watie grew increasingly weary of the diplomatic game and anxious about his destitute followers at home. He returned to his refugee family in the Choctaw Nation in May 1866. Stand Watie lost a son, his home, and his livelihood during the war. In the following years, misfortune plagued the Waties as two more sons died and their business ventures failed. Stand Watie spent his last years struggling to finance his children's education and restoring his pre-war home at Honey Springs. He died there on September 9, 1871. His courageous wife **Sarah** died twelve years later, outliving her remaining children.[26]

Hannah Hicks endured wartime trauma as a civilian and then suffered a further blow when her second husband, **Dr. Dwight Hitchcock,** died while tending smallpox patients after the war. She remained in the Cherokee Nation, serving as a distinguished representative of the pre-war generation.[27]

John Drew, ever remembered for the defection of his men, remained true to the Confederate cause despite hardships. The Confederate government hired him to transport food to the pro-Southern refugees but delayed payment for the saltworks which it had seized. Drew died in August 1865 while his wife and children remained as refugees in the Chickasaw Nation.[28]

Notes

INTRODUCTION

Epigraph: John Rollin Ridge to Stand Watie, October 9, [1854?] in Dale and Litton, *Cherokee Cavaliers*, 82.
　1. Elizabeth Watts, 11:289; Rachel Lane, 78:189, Indian Pioneer Papers, (hereafter cited as IPP; all material from this collection is personal narrative), Oklahoma Historical Society, Oklahoma City (hereafter cited as OHS).
　2. For examples of a broad-based approach, see Hauptman, *Between Two Fires*, and White and White, *Now the Wolf Has Come*.
　3. McLoughlin, *After the Trail of Tears*, 68.
　4. Elias C. Boudinot, 1866, quoted in McLoughlin, *After the Trail of Tears*, 223.
　5. Many more Cherokees achieved literacy in Cherokee via the amazing syllabary created by Sequoyah. Newspapers and government business were usually printed in both languages.
　6. Sturm, *Blood Politics*, 43.
　7. Champagne, *Social Order and Political Change*, 24.
　8. Hudson, *Southeastern Indians*, 266–67. Theda Perdue explains that this division of labor involved far more than simply economic allocation of resources in Perdue, *Cherokee Women*, 18.

9. Debo, *Road to Disappearance*, 15–17.

10. Champagne, *American Indian Societies*, 4, 9–10.

11. Alvin Josephy, *500 Nations*, 322; Evans, "Highways to Progress," 394–96.

12. Hudson, *Southeastern Indians*, 436; Perdue, *Cherokee Editor*, 5; Perdue, *Cherokee Women*, 23–24, 111; Saunt, *A New Order of Things*, 152.

13. Sturm, *Blood Politics*, 41.

14. Wardell, *Political History of the Cherokee Nation*, 99.

15. Perdue, "The Conflict Within," 62. Saunt, *A New Order of Things*, devotes several chapters to a discussion of the "Scots Indians'" role in changing Creek society. See Warde, *George Washington Grayson and the Creek Nation*, for the influence of mixed bloods in the region.

16. Berkhofer, *Salvation and the Savage*, 70–71.

17. White, *Roots of Dependency*, 120.

18. Perdue, "The Conflict Within," 60. Chief Charles Hicks set an example for his people by accepting baptism as a Moravian in 1813; see Ruff, "Notable Persons in Cherokee History: Charles Hicks," 18. For an understanding of the traditional Cherokee belief system, see Hudson, *Southeastern Indians*, Chapter 3.

19. In the 1850s, only two full-blood girls attended the Cherokee Female Seminary. See Mihesuah, *Cultivating the Rosebuds*, 40.

20. On the eve of the Civil War, the Cherokee Nation had 1,500 students enrolled in 30 public schools. See the report of H. D. Reese, Superintendent Public Schools, Cherokee Nation, in Commissioner of Indian Affairs, *Annual Report of the Commissioner of Indian Affairs, 1859* (hereafter cited as AR CIA and year), 177–78. At the other end of the spectrum, the Seminoles had no operating schools in 1859.

21. Report of Elias Rector, September 24, 1860, AR CIA 1860, 115.

22. Littlefield, *Cherokee Freedmen*, 9. No generalizations hold true in all cases; however, most men representing the tribes to the federal government were quite acculturated.

CHAPTER 1

Epigraph: Treaty of New Echota, Article 1, December 29, 1835, reprinted in Kappler, *Indian Affairs*, 2:440.

1. Jefferson wrote this in 1820. Its implications are examined in Fehrenbacher, "The Missouri Controversy and the Source of Southern Separatism," 653–57.

2. Wallace, *Long and Bitter Trail*, 52–4.

3. Wardell, *Political History of the Cherokee Nation*, 9. Elias Boudinot, the younger brother of Stand Watie, was born Buck Watie but changed his name to honor a white philanthropist who granted his education at a mission school in Connecticut.

4. Perdue, "The Conflict Within," 66–70.

5. John Ridge and Stand Watie, in Washington at the time, signed later.

6. Mooney, *Myths of the Cherokees*, 123.

7. Hagan, *American Indians*, 77.

8. Thornton, "Cherokee Population Loss During the Trail of Tears, 289–300.

9. Foreman, *Five Civilized Tribes*, 289; Moulton, *John Ross*, 149–50. See Agnew, *Fort Gibson*, for a full description of the terminus of the trail.

10. The problems of other tribes also plagued the Cherokees as the Seminoles' refusal to move into Creek territory left them in the Cherokee Nation until 1856.

11. Royce, "The Cherokee Nation of Indians," 202.

12. See Perdue, *Slavery and the Evolution of Cherokee Society, 1540–1866*, for a deeper understanding of the role slavery played in Cherokee society.

13. Perdue, *Slavery and the Evolution of Cherokee Society*, 50.

14. Perdue, *"Mixed Blood" Indians*, 5; Sturm, *Blood Politics*, 50.

15. Perdue, *Slavery and the Evolution of Cherokee Society*, 58.

16. Foreman, *A Traveler in Indian Territory*, 49.

17. Saunt, *A New Order of Things*, 109.

18. Littlefield, *Cherokee Freedmen*, 13n10. Estimates of slave ownership vary considerably. Littlefield places the number of Cherokee slaves in 1860 at 2,511, while William McLoughlin claims 4,000. See McLoughlin, "Red Indians, Black Slavery and White Racism," 380. Part of the difference may be that McLoughlin uses Cherokee Agent George Butler's report to the Commissioner in 1859, which mentioned 4,000 "negroes," all of whom may not have been slaves.

19. McLoughlin, *After the Trail of Tears*, 121.

20. Foreman, *Five Civilized Tribes*, 83. McLoughlin provides a helpful list of the restrictive laws passed in the Cherokee Nation in "Red Indians, Black Slavery and White Racism," 381.

21. Littlefield, *Cherokee Freedmen*, 9; Britton, *Memoirs of the Rebellion on the Border, 1863*, 142.

22. It is true that Creeks claimed as slaves black people who lived freely among the Seminoles, but that may be viewed as part of a larger power struggle. See Lancaster, *Removal Aftershock*, 28, 41.

23. McLoughlin, "Red Indians, Black Slavery and White Racism," 375; Hutchins, "The Trial of Reverend Samuel A. Worcester," 356–74; Bass, *Cherokee Messenger*, 154.

24. McLoughlin, *Cherokees and Christianity, 1794–1870*, 45.

25. Moore, *A Brief History of the Missionary Work in the Indian Territory of the Indian Mission Conference, Methodist Episcopal Church South*, 45.

26. James Anderson Slover autobiography, Western History Collection, University of Oklahoma, Norman, Oklahoma (hereafter cited as WHC); Israel Folsom to Cyrus Kingsbury, May 1, 1848, folder 9, Cyrus Kingsbury Collection (hereafter cited as CKC), WHC; John Edwards, "An Account of My Escape from the South in 1861," Thomas Gilcrease Institute of American History and Art, Tulsa, Oklahoma (hereafter cited as TGI); Charles Cutler Torrey autobiography, OHS.

27. Israel Folsom to Cyrus Kingsbury, May 1, 1848, folder 9; Cyrus Kingsbury to Board, July 17, 1858; Cyrus Kingsbury to Board, April 14, 1849, folder 5, CKC, WHC.

28. Cyrus Kingsbury to Board, December 27, 1853; Kingsbury to Board, April 5, 1859; Kingsbury to Board, April 30, 1851, folder 5, CKC, WHC.

29. Elizabeth Backus to ABCFM, May 8, 1854; Cyrus Kingsbury to Board, April 14, 1849, folder 5, CKC, WHC.

30. Cyrus Kingsbury to S. B. Treat; Cyrus Kingsbury to Board, February 1, 1854; Cyrus Kingsbury to Board, folder 5, CKC, WHC.

31. McLoughlin, *Champions of the Cherokees*, 290; Perdue, *Slavery and the Evolution of Cherokee Society*, 123; Arkansas Synod of Board of Foreign Missions to Secretary of Board, October 31, 1859, box 10, reel 1, American Indian Correspondence, WHC.

32. George Butler's report, AR CIA 1859, 172; George Butler to Charles Mix, October 12, 1858, reel 98, M234, RG75, National Archives, Washington, D.C. (hereafter cited as NA).

33. Franks, *Stand Watie and the Agony of the Cherokee Nation*, 114; Constitution of the Knights of the Golden Circle, August 28, 1860, Miscellaneous Documents Relating to Indian Affairs, John Vaughn Library, Northeastern University, Tahlequah, Oklahoma; William P. Adair to Stand Watie, August 29, 1861, file 5, box 153, Cherokee Nation Papers (hereafter cited as CNP), WHC.

34. The name has various spellings; the English version, Keetoowah, is one of the most common. The Cherokee word is the name of a conservative town in the old nation that apparently had a strong feeling of unity. See Mooney, *Myths of the Cherokee*, 225–26. The name is still in use in the Cherokee Nation, although the organization is different.

35. Wardell, *Political History of the Cherokees*, 121; McLoughlin, *Cherokees and Christianity*, 219.

36. Keetoowah constitution and laws reprinted in McLoughlin, *Cherokees and Christianity*, 244–53; see also Tyner, "The Keetoowah Society in Cherokee History." William P. Adair to Stand Watie, August 29, 1861, file 5, box 153, CNP, WHC; Mooney, *Myths of the Cherokee*, 226; Abel, *The American Indian as Slaveholder and Secessionist*, 68.

37. John Ross to J. S. Dunham, February 8, 1861, *Van Buren (Arkansas) Press*, in Moulton, *Papers of John Ross*, 2:458–59.

38. Letter of John Jones, September 12, 1860, quoted in McLoughlin, *Champions of the Cherokees*, 373; John Edwards (diary) collection, TGI; Cyrus Kingsbury to Board, April 11, 1860, folder 9, CKC, WHC.

39. John Ross to Henry Rector, February 22, 1861, frames 382–84, reel 100, M234, RG75, NA.

40. Mary Cobb Agnew, 66:23, IPP, WHC.

41. Morris, Goins, and McReynolds, *Historical Atlas of Oklahoma*, 7.

42. Pierce Butler's Report, September 30, 1843, AR CIA 1843.

43. Foreman, *A Traveler in Indian Territory*, 36.

44. George Butler's Report, September 10, 1859, AR CIA 1859.

45. *Cherokee Advocate*, September 2, 1851.

46. *Fort Smith Herald*, July 18, 1849.

47. *Cherokee Advocate*, May 22, 1845.

48. *Fort Smith Herald*, August 22, 1849.

49. *Cherokee Advocate*, March 6, 1845.

50. Governor Robert Walker spoke of Indian treaties as constituting "no obstacle" to the formation of a state from Indian Territory lands. See AR CIA 1857.

CHAPTER 2

Epigraph: John Ross to J. R. Kannady, May 17, 1861, frame 392, reel 100, M234, Correspondence of the Office of Indian Affairs, *Letters Received, 1824–81*, RG75, NA.

1. Henry Rector to John Ross, January 29, 1861, in U. S. War Department, *The War of the Rebellion: A Compilation of the Official Records of the Union and Confederate Armies*, ser. 1, vol. 1:683 (hereafter cited as *OR*, all references to series 1 unless otherwise noted). Mark Bean et al. to John Ross, May 9, 1861, frames 397–98; J. R. Kannady to John Ross, May 15, 1861, frame 388; and John Ross to J. R. Kannady, May 17, 1861, frame 392, reel 100, M234, RG75, NA.

2. Cyrus Harris to John Ross, January 5, 1861, reprinted in c69; William Ross to John Ross, frame 374, reel 100, M234, RG75, NA.

3. James Harrison to Edward Clark, April 23, 1861, *OR*, ser. 4, 1:322–25; David Hubbard to Andrew Moore, January 3, 1861, reprinted in Abel, *American Indian as Slaveholder*, 109–10; L. P. Walker to President Davis, April 27, 1861, *OR*, ser. 4, 1:248.

4. Nichols, *Lincoln and the Indians*, 27; Danziger, *Indians and Bureaucrats*, 168; Elias Rector to John Ross, February 14, 1861, frame 380, reel 100, M234, RG75, NA; Abel, *American Indian as Slaveholder*, 83; David Hubbard to John Ross and Ben McCulloch, June 12, 1861, OR, 13:497–98.

5. Abel, *American Indian as Slaveholder*, 101; B. Burroughs to Gov. C. Harris, May 8, 1861, *OR*, 1:691.

6. Wilson, "Delegates of the Five Civilized Tribes to the Confederate Congress," 353–66; Brown, *Life of Albert Pike*, 353–81; Abel, *American Indian as Slaveholder*, 160–77.

7. Wardell, *Political History of the Cherokee Nation*, 53.

8. Elias Boudinot to Stand Watie, October 5, 1861, file 8, box 149, CNP, WHC.

9. *OR*, ser. 4, 1:359–61.

10. Bahos, "John Ross: Unionist or Secessionist in 1861?" 172.

11. *OR*, 3:675.

12. The Confederate treaties are reprinted in Gibson, *Jefferson Davis and the Confederacy and Treaties Concluded by the Confederate States with the Indian Tribes*, 79–201.

13. Commissioner William Dole did write a letter to the chiefs, but the bearer, Superintendent William Coffin, was never able to establish a presence in Indian Territory. See Abel, *American Indian as Slaveholder*, 81.

14. Mary Cobb Agnew, 66:23, IPP, WHC.

15. Ella Coody Robinson, 107:465, IPP, OHS.

16. Davis, *The Cause Lost*, 84; Franks, *Stand Watie*, 182.

17. *OR*, 3:572, 574–75, 620.

18. *OR*, ser. 4, 1:360.

19. Chickasaw Governor Harris defined the Chickasaw goal of self-governance by claiming the right to hold "undisputed possessions of land and forts lately occupied by Federal forces and have the same garrisoned, if possible, by Chickasaw troops, or else by troops acting expressly under and by virtue of the authority of the Chickasaw or Choctaw nations." See Chickasaw Resolution, *OR*, 3:585, 1:648. African-American units, in contrast, could have only white officers. See Glatthaar, *Forged in Battle*, 35.

20. A. M. Wilson and J. W. Washbourne to Stand Watie, May 18, 1861, box 153, file 3, CNP.

21. W. P. Adair and James Bell to Stand Watie, August 29, 1861, in Dale and Litton, *Cherokee Cavaliers*, 108–110.

22. It was ironic that Ben McCulloch, who gained most of his military experience fighting Indians in his home state of Texas, was now welcoming Natives as valued military allies. See Cutrer, *Ben McCulloch and the Frontier Military Tradition*, 28, 48.

23. John Ross to Benjamin McCulloch, June 17, 1861, frames 407–10, reel 100, M234, RG75, NA.

24. *OR*, 3:692.

25. Jack Walton, 95:88, IPP, WHC; *OR* 3:54, 692, 690–91.

26. See Gaines, *The Confederate Cherokees*, 16–19, for a description of the regiment's officers.

27. James Bell to Col. Stand Watie, postscript, August 29, 1861, Watie miscellaneous box, CNP.

28. The issue was finally solved in 1862 when most of Drew's men defected to the Union army, leaving Watie's as the only Confederate Cherokee regiment. The *Official Records* standardize Drew as First Cherokee and Watie as Second Cherokee.

29. Abel, *The American Indian in the Civil War, 1862–1865*, 299.

30. Clark, "Opothleyahola and the Creeks during the Civil War," 50, 53; Charles Mix's report, AR CIA 1865, 328–30; Abel, *American Indian as Slaveholder*, 244.

31. For the text of the treaty, see *OR*, ser. 4, 1:426–43.

32. *OR*, 8:25; Opothleyahola and Ouktahnaserharjo to Abraham Lincoln, August 15, 1861, reprinted in Abel, *American Indian as Slaveholder*, 245–46, 248.

33. *OR*, 8:5; John Ross to Opothleyahola and other chiefs and headmen of the Creek Nation, September 19, 1861; Moty Kennard and Echo Harjo to John Ross, October 18, 1861, in Moulton, *Papers of Chief John Ross*, 2:487–88, 496–97.

34. *OR*, 8:5–14; Moty Kennard and Echo Harjo to Cooper, October 31, 1861, Creek National Records, OHS.

35. *OR*, 8:5.

36. Hale, "Rehearsal for Civil War," 235.

37. Mayberry, "Texans and the Defense of the Confederate Northwest," 215; *OR*, 8:15; Bearss, "The Civil War Comes to Indian Territory," 20.

38. *OR*, 8:6; Pascofar to President Lincoln, March 10, 1864, frame 154, reel 803, M234, RG75, NA; Bahos, "On Opothleyahola's Trail," 58–89, 61.

39. *OR* 8:7; Gaines, *Confederate Cherokees*, 45–47. John Ross later pardoned these deserters, and many returned to Confederate service for a short time.

40. Gaines, *Confederate Cherokees*, 46.

41. *OR*, 8:18.

42. Trickett, "The Civil War in Indian Territory, 1861," 266; *OR*, 8:8.

43. Hale, "Rehearsal for Civil War," 244; Fischer and Franks, "Confederate Victory at Chusto-Talasah," 475. Cooper estimated five hundred dead; Col. D. N. McIntosh counted only twenty-seven bodies.

44. *OR*, 8:11, 13.

45. *OR*, 8:23.

46. The weather was so bad that one of Cooper's men froze to death, a light loss compared to the sufferings of the ill-supplied Creeks.

47. *OR*, 8:24, 31.

48. Gary Gallagher, keynote speech (annual meeting of Society of Civil War Historians, Houston, Texas, November 7, 2003).

49. Cottrell, *Civil War in the Indian Territory*, 14.

50. Brown, *Life of Albert Pike*, 375.

51. John Ross to Albert Pike, February 25, 1862, in Moulton, *Papers of Chief John Ross*, 2:509; *OR*, 8:287.

52. McPherson, *Atlas of the Civil War*, 48–49.

53. Earl J. Hess and William L. Shea claim that Indians were not involved in the attack on the Union artillery. See Hess and Shea, *Pea Ridge*, 101. However, this seems to contradict the report of Union Colonel Peter J. Osterhaus who noted "a great many Indians" among the cavalry who overwhelmed him. See *OR*, 8:217. See also Britton, *The Civil War on the Border*, 247.

54. Britton, *The Union Indian Brigade in the Civil War*, 55.

55. Monaghan, *Civil War on the Western Border*, 246.

56. Ibid., 249.

57. *OR*, 8:217, 233–34; Brown, *A Life of Albert Pike*, 390–94.

CHAPTER 3

Epigraph: Albert Pike to Stand Watie, April 1, 1862, in Dale and Litton, *Cherokee Cavaliers*, 116.

1. *OR*, 8:286, 13:815.
2. Ella Coody Robinson, 107:466, IPP, OHS.
3. One such encounter occurred at Neosho, Missouri, in April 1862.
4. *OR*, 8:282; Gaines, *Confederate Cherokees*, 91.
5. Ross to Pike, March 22, 1862, in Moulton, *Papers of Chief John Ross*, 2:510–11. Ross complained of "the unwarrantable conduct" of some of Watie's men. See Ross to Pike, February 25, 1862, ibid., 2:509.
6. See Hauptman, *Between Two Fires*, for the difficulties encountered by tribal members in joining the army.
7. Abel, *American Indian in the Civil War*, 99, 114; *OR*, 13:365; Coffin, AR CIA 1862, 136–37.
8. Heath, "The First Federal Invasion of Indian Territory," 410, 412–13.
9. *OR*, 13:487.
10. *OR*, 13:430.
11. Monaghan, *Civil War on the Western Border*, 253; *OR*, 13:430, 487.
12. Britton, *Union Indian Brigade*, 65.
13. *OR*, 13:475–76, 485.
14. Gaines, *Confederate Cherokees*, 48.
15. *OR*, 13:950
16. Moulton, *John Ross*, 174.
17. Britton, *Union Indian Brigade*, 69–72.
18. *OR*, 13:488.
19. *OR*, 13:512, 478.
20. *OR*, 13:473.
21. Stand Watie to Douglass Cooper, February 2, 1862, in Dale and Litton, *Cherokee Cavaliers*, 112
22. *OR*, 13:162; John Ross to Abraham Lincoln, September 16, 1862; Whitecatcher et al. and Daniel Ross to John Ross, December 2, 1862, in Moulton, *Papers of Chief John Ross*, 2:517, 522–23.
23. Moulton, *John Ross*, 175, 143.
24. *OR*, 13:486.
25. Lincoln to Ross, September 25, 1862 in Basler, *Collected Works of Abraham Lincoln*, 5:440.
26. Moulton, *John Ross*, 177.

27. Pike in fact was arrested and resigned twice before he finally left the army for good in November, 1862.

28. *OR*, 22 (2):60–62.

29. Britton, *Union Indian Brigade*, 89.

30. Ibid., 95.

31. Ibid., 103.

32. *OR*, 22 (1):83.

33. *OR*, 22 (2):85.

34. Britton, *Union Indian Brigade*, 202.

35. Ibid., 212.

36. Ella Coody Robinson, 107:472, IPP, OHS.

37. *OR*, 22 (2):770.

38. The Union renamed Fort Gibson as Fort Blunt in May 1863 and then changed it back in December. See Foreman, *Fort Gibson*, 36.

39. Franks, *Stand Watie and the Agony of the Cherokee Nation*, 136–37.

40. *OR*, 22 (1): 381.

41. Monaghan, *Civil War on the Western Border*, 278.

42. Cottrell, *Civil War in the Indian Territory*, 78.

43. *OR*, 22 (1):33; Britton, *Memoirs of the Rebellion on the Border*, 361. These two sources report widely varying numbers of wounded.

44. D. H. Cooper to James M. Bell, September 24, 1863, in Dale and Litton, *Cherokee Cavaliers*, 141; E. J. (probably Evan Jones, Baptist missionary) to John Ross, July 21, 1863, John Ross Papers, TGI.

45. Stand Watie to Sarah C. Watie, November 12, 1863, in Dale and Litton, *Cherokee Cavaliers*, 144–45; Edward Butler to Cousin, July 3, 1863, reprinted in "Notes and Documents," *Chronicles of Oklahoma* 44 (1966):322–23.

46. Bearss and Gibson, *Fort Smith*, 284; Lee, "The Capture of the J. R. Williams," 22–33.

47. Grayson, *A Creek Warrior for the Confederacy*, 82–87; *OR*, 34 (1):1012.

48. Bearss and Gibson, *Fort Smith*, 288; Hood, "Twilight of the Confederacy in Indian Territory," 437; letter, no date, Richard Martin Collection, WHC; William McComb memoirs, Section X-Civil War, OHS.

49. General S. B. Maxey apparently believed that by continuing to destroy Federal supplies, he would force them to abandon the forts. *OR*, 41 (1):1035.

50. Grayson, *A Creek Warrior for the Confederacy*, 66.

51. Edward Butler to Cousin, July 3, 1863, reprinted in "Notes and Documents," *Chronicles of Oklahoma* 44 (Fall 1966): 322–23; Grayson, *A Creek Warrior for the Confederacy*, 66; Captain B. W. Marston inspection

report, December 1864, original in Archives Division of the Louisiana State University, Baton Rouge, reprinted in Ashcraft, "Confederate Troop Conditions in 1864," 443–45.

52. *OR*, 22 (2):1094; *OR*, 22 (1):35. Indian leaders generally disliked Steele. See Elias Boudinot to Stand Watie, January 24, 1864; and William Steele to Stand Watie, April 21, 1864, Dale and Litton, *Cherokee Cavaliers*, 151, 154.

53. Horton, *Samuel Bell Maxey*, 35–43; Abel, *American Indian in the Civil War*, 313; Franzmann, "The Final Campaign: The Confederate Offensive of 1864," 268.

54. Cooper and Maxey clashed repeatedly in their short relationship. See *OR*, 34 (4):698.

55. *OR*, 41 (2):1019; *OR*, (3):971; *OR*, 48 (1)·1408. The machinations of Douglas Cooper in his attempt to gain power are exposed in the papers of Samuel B. Maxey, 93–115, TGI.

CHAPTER 4

Epigraph: Hannah Hicks diary, November 17, 1862, TGI.

1. The alleged "barbarities" took place away from the center of the fighting, in an area where officers exercised little control during the battle. See Hess and Shea, *Pea Ridge*, 357n32.

2. Hale, "Rehearsal for Civil War," 228–65; Britton, *Civil War on the Border*, 275; Abel, *American Indian in the Civil War*, 31n65, 33; *OR*, 8:194, 207, 288, 820.

3. *OR*, 8:195.

4. Gibson, *The Chickasaws*, 43.

5. *OR*, 3:625; *OR*, 13:826; Davis, *The Cause Lost*, 90–91.

6. On the other hand, Indians also exhibited racism in their encounters with black troops. Watie's men slaughtered members of the First Kansas Colored Infantry at Prairie Springs. See Davis, *The Cause Lost*, 71, 85–86.

7. *OR*, 34 (4):699–700.

8. *OR*, 22:35; Captain B. W. Marston report, December 1864, in Ashcraft, "Confederate Indian Troop Conditions," 446; *OR*, 34 (4):699.

9. *OR*, 34 (4):701.

10. *OR*, 13:819.

11. Some white men tried to join Indian regiments in order to avoid discipline. See *OR*, 22 (2):1104.

12. Captain B. W. Marston report, December 1864, Ashcraft, "Confederate Indian Troop Conditions," 445.

13. *OR*, 22 (1):28–29.

14. Pike was the Indian soldiers' greatest supporter, and Choctaws and Chickasaws petitioned Richmond to give D. H. Cooper command of Indian Territory.

15. S. B. Maxey report, November 6, 1864, #160, Samuel B. Maxey Papers, TGI; *OR*, 34 (1):841; *OR*, 53:963–66.

16. *OR*, 34 (4):701.

17. *OR*, 13:93; Britton, *Memoirs of the Rebellion on the Border*, 201; Grayson, *A Creek Warrior for the Confederacy*, 93–94.

18. Britton, *Union Indian Brigade*, 188.

19. Abel, *American Indian in the Civil War*, 109; *OR*, 22 (2):1112; *OR*, 22:34.

20. *OR*, 13: 820, 846, 858, 860, 938; Albert Pike to Major General Theophilus Holmes, December 30, 1862, in Abel, *American Indian in Civil War*, 337; Britton, *The Union Indian Brigade*, 61; Britton, *Memoirs of the Rebellion on the Border*, 200; Emiziah Bohanon, 1:222, IPP, OHS.

21. *OR*, 13:950: "The Indian troops who have been true to the South from the very first have been treated in many instances as though it were immaterial whether or not they were paid as promptly and equipped as thoroughly as other soldiers. Money specially obtained for them has more than once been appropriated to the use of other commands. Clothing, procured at great trouble and expense, to cover the nakedness of Indian troops, has on several occasions been distributed among less necessitous soldiers." Stand Watie to S. S. Scott, *OR*, 22 (2):1104–105; Captain B. W. Marston report, December 1864, in Ashcraft, "Confederate Indian Troop Conditions," 446.

22. *OR*, 22 (2):1104–05; *OR*, 54:954.

23. *OR*, 8:286–92.

24. The muster rolls and reports in the Union army completed by white officers duly reported absent men as deserted or absent without leave. In the southern system, which had far more Indian officers, men are referred to in officers' correspondence as being on furlough.

25. #131, 1st Indian Home Guard, Compiled Service Records, AGO, RG94, NA; Pension record of Samuel Yahola, Co. E., 3rd Indian Home Guard, NA; Individual pension records, #517626, NA. The corresponding Confederate records are not complete.

26. Muster Roll, company "F," 3rd Indian Home Guard Regiment, OHS.

27. Britton, *Memoirs of the Rebellion on the Border*, 131, 176; *OR*, 22 (2):61; McPherson, *Battle Cry of Freedom*, 487.

28. Mitchell, *Civil War Soldiers*, 75, 24–25.

29. On Missouri's travail, see especially Fellman, *Inside War*.

30. Numerous white families illegally encroached on Indian land, especially on the Cherokees' northern holdings.

31. The Worcesters, Robertsons, Hitchcocks, and Foremans were a well-known, interconnected missionary group.

32. Major B. S. Henning to Col. U. P. Chipman, November 25, 1862, reel 6, M825, RG48, NA.

33. Alice Robertson, "Incidents of the Civil War," Alice Robertson Papers, box 1, OHS.

34. Hannah Hicks diary, August 17, 1862, TGI.

35. Stand, the Cherokee who killed Hicks, was a complete stranger.

36. Hannah Hicks diary, September 7, 1862, TGI.

37. Ibid., September 14, 1862, n. 5; Foreman, "Reverend Stephen Foreman: Cherokee Missionary," 229–42; Stephen Foreman journal, January 1864, Stephen Foreman Collection, WHC.

38. Hannah Hicks diary, August 24, 1862, TGI.

39. Isaac Hitchcock journal, April 20, 1861, and February 1862, TGI.

40. Mary Jane Rider, 76:161, IPP, WHC; Hannah Hicks diary, November 16, 1862, TGI.

41. Foreman, *Park Hill*, 136; *OR*, 13:161, 138.

42. Franks, *Stand Watie and the Agony of the Cherokee Nation*, 129; Abel, *American Indian in the Civil War*, 193.

43. Ash, *When the Yankees Came*, 104.

44. Hannah Hicks diary, December 9 and February 20, 1863, TGI.

45. Ibid., September 5, October 27, and November 10, 1862; Isaac Hitchcock journal, December 3, 1861, TGI; Mary Jane Rider, 76:161, IPP, WHC.

46. Hannah Hicks to sister, September 16, 1865, box 3, folder 3, Grant Foreman Collection, Gilcrease Institute.

47. Hannah Hicks diary, September 16, 1862, and December 23, 1862, TGI.

48. Hannah Hicks observed that "The Pins have been robbing some of their enemies." Ibid., November 7, 1862.

49. Ibid., November 17, 1862.

50. Ibid., note 9, note 7; Samantha Lane Hillen, George Mayes, 42:410, 61:302, IPP, WHC.

51. In 1861, Indian Territory was reported to "have an immense supply of beeves, sufficient to supply the meat for the whole Confederate service." *OR*, 3:589.

52. Rider, 76:161, IPP, WHC.

53. Hannah Hicks diary, September 20, 1862, TGI; Hannah Worcester Hitchcock to A. E. W. Robertson, May 12, 1863, file 133, box 9, Robertson Papers, University of Tulsa, Tulsa, Oklahoma.

54. Lizzie Clark to A. E. W. Robertson, January 20, 1863, Robertson Papers, University of Tulsa; Hannah Hicks diary, January 1, 1863, TGI.

55. Hannah Hicks diary, September 28, 1862, TGI.

56. Ash, *When the Yankees Came*, 93. For examples of Native interest in the broader war, see Hannah Hicks diary, September 14, October 5, and November 18, 1862, TGI.

CHAPTER 5

Epigraph: Sarah Watie to Stand Watie, May 20, 1863, box 147, folder 5, CNP, WHC.

1. Monaghan, *Civil War on the Western Border*, 220–21; *James Scott*, 9:172, IPP, OHS; Debo, *Road to Disappearance*, 151.

2. Agent John Jones, April 7, 1873, quoted in Abel, *American Indian as Slaveholder*, 268–9.

3. *Webster's New Collegiate Dictionary*, s.v. "Refugees."

4. Joseph Bruner, 89:266, IPP, OHS; Monaghan, *Civil War on the Western Border*, 227; Debo, *Road to Disappearance*, 151–52.

5. Joseph Bruner, 89:266, IPP, OHS.

6. George A. Cutler's report, AR CIA 1862, 139.

7. The refugee count varies by source and date. Most sources point to more than three thousand people traveling with Opothleyahola, but the number of refugees in Kansas increased monthly in 1862, surpassing seven thousand. See AR CIA 1862, 1, 27, 157.

8. William Coffin's report, AR CIA 1862, 136; William P. Dole's report, AR CIA 1862, 25; George Cutler's report, AR CIA 1862, 139.

9. Dole, AR CIA 1862, 26; Cutler, AR CIA 1862, 139; A. B. Campbell's report, AR CIA 1862, 153–54.

10. Coffin estimated 1,200 to 1,500 dead ponies around the camps and in the river. See February 13, 1862, AR CIA 1862, 145.

11. Coffin reported twenty to sixty people still coming in every day in February 1862. Ibid.

12. George W. Collamore's report, AR CIA 1862, 156; Coffin to Dole, February 13, 1862, frame 1117, reel 834, M234, RG75, NA.

13. For example, the military relocated Cherokee refugees to Neosho without the approval of Indian Superintendent Coffin. See Coffin to Mix, August 31, 1863, frame 310, reel 835, M234, RG75, NA.

14. Coffin, AR CIA 1862, 136; Dole, AR CIA 1862, 148; David Hunter, AR CIA 1862, 150.

15. Coffin, AR CIA 1862, 136.

16. Coffin to Dole, February 13, 1862, frame 1115, reel 834, M234, RG75, NA.

17. Coffin to Dole, June 6, 1863, frame 229, reel 835, M234, RG75, NA.

18. Dole, AR CIA 1862, 154–55,

19. Coffin, AR CIA 1862, 147.

20. Kansas residents found a sympathetic ear in Washington when they filed claims against the tribes for alleged depredations committed by refugees. United States Commissioner of Indian Affairs William Dole stated that "there is little doubt that many depredations . . . have been perpetrated by Indians." Dole to William Otto, Assistant Sec. of Interior, May 29, 1863, reel 13, M348, Correspondence of the Office of Indian Affairs, Report Books, 1838–85, RG75, NA.

21. Collamore, AR CIA 1862, 156; George A. Cutler, AR CIA 1862, 139.

22. Dole, AR CIA 1862, 155; G. A. Snow, AR CIA 1862, 142.

23. Cutler, AR CIA 1862, 140.

24. Colonel Ross to Coffin, May 26, 1863, frames 204–17, reel 834, M234, RG75, NA.

25. Henry Smith to Coffin, July 16, 1863, frames 275, reel 834, M234, RG75, NA.

26. Proctor to Coffin, November 26, 1863, frame 383, reel 835, M234, RG75, NA.

27. Harlan to Coffin, August 8, 1863, frames 287–91, reel 835, M234, RG75, NA.

28. John Ross to Annie B. Ross, September 18, 1865, in Moulton, *Papers of Chief John Ross*, 2:649; Abel, *American Indian and the End of the Confederacy*, 61–67.

29. Fischer and McMurray, "Confederate Refugees From Indian Territory," 452.

30. Woodward, *The Cherokees*, 283–86; Gibson, *The Chickasaws*, 271; Baird, *Peter Pitchlynn*, 137; Debo, *Rise and Fall of the Choctaw Republic*, 92.

31. The Confederacy and the individual tribes did allot funds for the purchase of refugee rations, but the people were not contained in a few camps with regular distribution as they were in Kansas.

32. Elinor Boudinot Meigs, 7:179A, IPP, OHS; Jim Spaniard, 86:14, Betsy Christie, 18:84, IPP, WHC.

33. Andy Cordray, 20:81, Elsie Edwards, 27:190, Minnie Wimberley Hodge, 43:107, Betsy Christie, 18:82, IPP, WHC.

34. Polly Barnett, 5:401, Jim Spaniard, 86:14, Eliza Breeding, 11:12, IPP, WHC.

35. Richard Fields Boudinot, 1:225, IPP, OHS; Christopher Columbus Choat, 18:5, Martha Walker Gibson, 94:376, IPP, WHC; *OR*, 53:1035.

36. Mary Mackay Wilson 99:53, IPP, WHC.

37. Eliza Adair, T-663, Doris Duke Oral History Collection, WHC; E. F. Dodson, 3:80, IPP, OHS.

38. Sarah Watie to Stand Watie, May 20, 1862, file 5, box 147; Nancy Starr to Sarah C. Watie, July 24, 1854, file 22, box 155, CNP, WHC.

39. See Perdue, *Cherokee Women*, for a fuller explanation of the role of matrilineality in Cherokee society.

40. James Bell to Stand Watie, July 24, 1854, file 2, box 170, CNP, WHC.

41. In May 1863, she proposed buying a house for $3,000. Sarah C. Watie to Stand Watie, May 20, 1863, file 5, box 147, CNP, WHC.

42. Mary Starr to James Bell, June 22, 1864, file 25, box 170; Sarah C. Watie to Stand Watie, May 20, 1863, file 5, box 147, CNP, WHC.

43. Carolyn Johnston argues that this focus on morality reflects elite Cherokee women's commitment to the cult of true womanhood. More likely it reveals the nature of tribal community life where clan and family ties ensure proper behavior and mete out punishment for offenses. The Watie family had paid dearly two decades previously for transgressing the will of the community. See Johnston, *Cherokee Women in Crisis*, 97.

44. Sarah C. Watie to Stand Watie, May 20, 1863, file 5; June 8, 1863, file 6; May 20, 1863, file 5; and August 21, 1863, file 8, box 147, CNP, WHC.

45. Massey, *Refugee Life in the Confederacy*; Sarah C. Watie to Stand Watie, May 20, 1863, file 5, September 4, 1864, file 17, box 147, CNP, WHC.

46. Sarah C. Watie to Stand Watie, May 21, 1865, file 22, box 147, CNP, WHC; Gibson, *The Chickasaws*, 270.

47. Debo, *Rise and Fall of the Choctaw Republic*, 91.

48. For studies of southern women in wartime see Clinton, *The Other Civil War*; Faust, *Mothers of Invention*; and Rable, *Civil Wars: Women and the Crisis of Southern Nationalism.*

49. One measure of the extent to which individuals have moved from traditional customs to Euro-American cultural norms is adherence to Christianity. In 1860 only about 12 percent of Cherokees claimed membership in Christian churches. See McLoughlin, *Cherokees and Missionaries*, 337.

50. Faust, "Altars of Sacrifice," 1220–28; Johnston, *Cherokee Women in Crisis*, 102.

51. Sarah Watie to Stand Watie, June 12, 1864, Watie Papers, box 115, folder 3899, WHC.

52. Littlefield, *Chickasaw Freedmen*, 18; ibid., 9.

53. Berlin, *Slaves No More*, 4.

54. Jim Tomm, John Harrison, 91:323, 39:329, IPP, WHC.

55. Wm. Ross to Col. Cooper, August 18, 1862, Cherokee Collection, Miscellaneous Letters, John Vaughn Library, Northeastern State University, Tahlequah, Oklahoma.

56. Berlin, *Slaves No More*, 16.

57. Narrative of J. W. Stinnett, in Rawick, *The American Slave*, 12:296.

58. Berlin, *Slaves No More*, 2.

59. Narrative of Victoria Taylor Thompson; narrative of Patsy Perryman, in Rawick, *The American Slave*, 12:320, 252.

60. Narrative of Ed Butler, ibid., 12:88.

61. Elsie Garner, 3:129, IPP, WHC.

62. Ash, *When the Yankees Came*, 163.

63. Sarah Watie to Stand Watie, May 20, 1863, file 5, box 147, CNP; narrative of Jim Threat, in Rawick, *The American Slave*, 12:329, 331; Berlin, *Slaves No More*, 13.

64. Berlin, *Slaves No More*, 34; Isaac Hitchcock journal, July 7, 1862, TGI; narrative of Lonian Moses, in Rawick, *The American Slave*, 12:210–11.

65. Eliza Hardrick, 38:322, IPP, WHC.

66. Dennis Vann, 11:66, IPP, WHC; Halliburton, *Red Over Black*, 129.

67. Jim Tomm, 91:323, IPP, WHC; narrative of Rochelle Allred Ward; narrative of Richard Franklin, in Rawick, *The American Slave*, 12:359, 133.

68. Narrative of Jim Threat; narrative of Patsy Perryman, in Rawick, *The American Slave*, 12:338, 252.

69. Abel, *American Indian and the End of the Confederacy*, 363.

EPILOGUE

Epigraph: D. N. Cooley, AR CIA 1865, 38.

1. For an overview of the Reconstruction period, see Foner, *Reconstruction*.

2. Royce, "The Cherokee Nation of Indians," 351, 376; Dole, AR CIA 1865, 38–9; Coffin, AR CIA 1863, 176; Kensell, "Phases of Reconstruction in the Choctaw Nation, 1865–1870," 138; Hammond, "Socioeconomic Reconstruction in the Cherokee Nation, 1865–1870," 159.

3. Elijah Sells, 260; George Reynolds, 282; Justin Harlan, 285; and J. W. Dunn, 291, in AR CIA 1865.

4. E. Jane Ross to John Ross, December 21, 1864, in Moulton, *Papers of Chief John Ross*, 2:614.

5. Moulton, *Papers of Chief John Ross*, 2:596.

6. Harriman, "Economic Conditions in the Creek Nation, 1865–71," 326; Sells, AR CIA 1865, 252–53. Colonel William Phillips accused Superintendent William Coffin, his agents, and indirectly Commissioner William Dole of complicity in the cattle thefts. All those accused denied any improper behavior and the matter died. See AR CIA 1865, 272–79.

7. James Dunn's report 291; Elijah Sells's report, 260, AR CIA 1865.

8. Dale and Litton, *Cherokee Cavaliers*, 230; Elijah Sells's report, 254–56, 260; Isaac Coleman's report, 280, AR CIA 1865.

9. Contract, September 1, 1863, John Drew Papers, TGI; Baird, *A Creek Warrior*, 164.

10. Gaines, *Confederate Cherokees*, 124, claims that the Union Indian soldiers suffered a higher percentage of deaths than soldiers from any state. He bases this on figures of 3,530 enlistees and 1,018 deaths, a 28.8 percent rate of loss.

11. McCullar, "The Choctaw-Chickasaw Reconstruction Treaty of 1866," in Fischer, *Civil War Era in Indian Territory*, 338; Abel, *American Indian and the End of the Confederacy*, 337; Miner, *The Corporation and the Indian*, 11.

12. Abel, *American Indian and the End of the Confederacy*, 240, 301.

13. AR CIA 1865, 304.

14. Ibid., 306, 312.

15. Abel, *American Indian and the End of the Confederacy*, 329. Debo calls the treaty a "triumph of diplomacy." See Debo, *Rise and Fall of the Choctaw Republic*, 87.

16. Seminole Treaty of 1866 in Kappler, *Indian Affairs*, 2:911; Bailey, *Reconstruction in Indian Territory*, 76; Morton, "Reconstruction in the Creek Nation," 173.

17. The Southern Cherokee delegation strongly represented the old feud over the Removal Treaty. Stand Watie, who survived the assassination attempts, and his son were joined by E. C. Boudinot and John Rollin Ridge, the sons of two men who were killed that day in 1839.

18. Lambert, "The Cherokee Reconstruction Treaty of 1866," in Fischer, *Civil War Era in Indian Territory*, 146.

19. J. W. Washbourne to J.A. Scales, June 1, 1866, in Dale and Litton, *Cherokee Cavaliers*, 245.

20. Royce, "The Cherokee Nation of Indians," 347; Thoburn, "The Cherokee Question," 141–242; Warren, "Reconstruction in the Cherokee Nation," 180–89; Lambert, "The Cherokee Reconstruction Treaty of 1866," 142–50.

21. Elias C. Boudinot to John Rollin Ridge, box 152, CNP, WHC.

22. Kappler, *Indian Affairs*, 2:942–44.

23. The story of freedpeople in Indian Territory is an important one. See especially the work of Daniel Littlefield, Jr. in *Africans and Seminoles*, *The Cherokee Freedmen*, *Africans and Creeks*, and *The Chickasaw Freedmen*. See also May, *African Americans and Native Americans in the Creek and Cherokee Nations*; and Wilson, "Freedmen in Indian Territory During Reconstruction," 230–44.

24. The proceedings at Fort Smith are recorded in AR CIA 1865, 312–53. The final treaties signed in Washington in 1866 are reprinted in Kappler, *Indian Affairs*, 2:910–42.

25. Moulton, *John Ross*, 189–95.

26. Franks, *Stand Watie*, 180, 190, 200, 208.

27. Wright, "Notes on the Life of Mrs. Hannah Worcester Hicks and the Park Hill Press," 350.

28. Contract, September 1, 1863, John Drew Papers, TGI.

Bibliography

ARCHIVES AND RECORDS

John Vaughn Library, Special Collections, Northeastern State University, Tahlequah, Oklahoma.
Cherokee Collection, Miscellaneous Letters.
Miscellaneous Documents Relating to Indian Affairs.
Watie Letters.
National Archives, Washington, D.C.
Records of the Adjutant General's Office, 1780s–1917, Record Group 94.
Compiled Records Showing Service of Military Units in Volunteer Union Organizations Microcopy 594, roll 225.
Records of the Bureau of Indian Affairs, Record Group 75.
Correspondence of the Office of Indian Affairs, Letters Received, 1824–1881. Microcopy 234, rolls 98–101, 142, 175–76, 196, 230–31, 803, 834–37.
Correspondence of the Office of Indian Affairs, Letters Sent, 1824–1881. Microcopy 21, rolls 64–78.
Correspondence of the Office of Indian Affairs, Registers of Letters Received, 1824–1880. Microcopy 18, rolls 54–68.

Correspondence of the Office of Indian Affairs, Report Books, 1838–1885. Microcopy 348, rolls 10–16, 27–28, 59, 75.

Correspondence of the Office of Indian Affairs, Special Files, 1807–1904. Microcopy 574, rolls 11, 24, 27, 28, 59.

Records of Southern Superintendency, 1832–1870. Microcopy 640, rolls 16, 21–22.

Records Relating to Claims Arising From Military Service of Indians During the Civil War.

List of Claimants, 1865–72.

Register of Admitted Pension Claims, by heirs and invalids, 1866–69.

Register of Pension Claims based on death or injury, 1873–75 - 550.

Register of Claims for Bounties and Back Pay, 1869–90.

Ledger for Accounts of E. B. Stover, guardian for minor heirs, 1869–70.

Records Concerning John Wright and Indian Home Guard Claims, 1865–75.

Index to Abstract List of Indian Applicants for Military Bounty Land, 1855–75.

Abstract of Claims.

Records of the Office of the Secretary of the Interior, Record Group 48.

Selected Classes of Letters Received by the Indian Division of the Office of Secretary of Interior, 1849–1880. Microcopy 825, rolls 6, 20–22.

Records of the Indian Division of the Office of Secretary of Interior, Letters Sent, 1849–1903. Microcopy 606, rolls 3–5.

Records of the Veterans Administration, Record Group 15.

Organizational Index to Pension Files of Veterans Who Served Between 1861 and 1900. Microcopy T 289, rolls 130–31.

War Department Collection of Confederate Records, Record Group 109.

Compiled Service Records of Confederate Soldiers Who Served in Organizations Raised Directly by the Confederate Government. Microcopy 258, rolls 77–91.

Compiled Records Showing Service of Military Units in Confederate Organizations. Microcopy 861, roll 74.

Oklahoma Historical Society Archives and Manuscripts Division, Oklahoma Historical Society, Oklahoma City, Oklahoma.

John T. Adair Papers.

Cyrus Byington Collection.
Cherokee National Records.
Choctaw National Records.
Choctaw and Chickasaw Observer.
Confederate Memorial Hall Records.
Creek National Records.
George Fine Papers.
Grant Foreman Collection.
Stephen Foreman Papers.
Indian Pioneer Papers.
2nd and 3rd Indian Regiment Roll Book.
Minutes of the Indian Mission Conference of the Methodist Episcopal
    Church, 1844–1877.
Gary Moulton Collection of John Ross Papers.
John Ross Papers.
Senseney Collection.
William Smith Papers.
Emmett Starr Papers.
Joseph Thoburn Papers.
Charles Cutler Torrey, autobiography.
George L. Washington Papers.
Stand Watie Journal.
Muriel Wright Papers.
Section X.
    Cherokees, Civil War.
    Creek, Civil War.
Thomas Gilcrease Institute of American History and Art, Tulsa, Okla-
    homa.
Cyrus Byington Papers.
Choctaw and Chickasaw Resolutions.
Confederate Papers.
John Drew Papers.
John Edwards Papers.
Grant Foreman Collection.
Isaac Hitchcock Journal.
Samuel B. Maxey Papers.
Peter Pitchlynn Papers.
John Ross Papers.
James Green Walker Diary.
Worcester Papers.

University of Tulsa, Tulsa, Oklahoma. Alice Robertson Papers.
Western History Collections, University of Oklahoma, Norman, Oklahoma.
  Cherokee Nation Papers.
  Colonial Dames Collection.
  Confederate States of America Indian Affairs Collection.
  William Elsey Connelly Papers.
  Creek Nation Papers.
  Edward Everett Dale Papers.
  Division of Manuscripts Collection.
  Doris Duke Oral History Collection.
  Alan W. Farley Papers.
  Stephen Foreman Papers.
  Arrell M. Gibson Papers.
  Grayson Family Papers.
  Jay L. Hargett Papers.
  James R. Hendricks Papers.
  Indian Pioneer Papers.
  Cyrus Kingsbury Papers.
  Mrs. John B. Lilley Papers.
  Richard L. Martin Papers.
  W. D. and James Morrison Papers.
  Peter Perkins Pitchlynn Papers.
  James Ross Ramsay Papers.
  John Ross Papers.
  Seminole Nation Papers.
  James Anderson Slover Papers.
  Silas Turnbo Papers.
  Tandy C. Walker Papers.
  Watie Boudinot Papers.
  Works Progress Administration Historic Sites and Federal Writers' Project Records Collection.

PUBLISHED DOCUMENTS

Ashcraft, Allan C., ed. "Confederate Indian Department Conditions in August 1864." *Chronicles of Oklahoma* 41 (Fall): 270–85.
———. "Confederate Troop Conditions in August 1864." *Chronicles of Oklahoma* 41 (Winter 1963–64):442–49.

———. "Confederate Indian Territory Conditions in 1865." *Chronicles of Oklahoma* 42 (Winter 1964–65):421–28.

Basler, Roy P., ed. *The Collected Works of Abraham Lincoln*. 9 vols. New Brunswick, N.J.: Rutgers University Press, 1953–55.

Berlin, Ira, Barbara Fields, Steven Miller, Joseph Reidy, and Leslie Rowland. *Free at Last: A Documentary History of Slavery, Freedom, and the Civil War*. New York: The New Press, 1992.

Blunt, James G. "General Blunt's Account of his Civil War Experiences." *Kansas Historical Quarterly* 1 (May 1932): 211–65.

Britton, Wiley. *Memoirs of the Rebellion on the Border, 1863*. 1882. Reprint, Lincoln: University of Nebraska Press, 1993.

———. *The Union Indian Brigade in the Civil War*. Ottawa, Kansas: Kansas Heritage Press, 1922.

Commissioner of Indian Affairs. *Report of the Commissioner of Indian Affairs*. 1859–66. Washington, D.C.: Government Printing Office, 1860–67.

Dale, Edward Everett, and Gaston Litton, eds. *Cherokee Cavaliers: Forty Years of Cherokee History as Told in the Correspondence of the Ridge-Watie-Boudinot Family*. Norman: University of Oklahoma Press, 1939.

Dale, Edward Everett, ed. "Some Letters of General Stand Watie." *Chronicles of Oklahoma* 1 (1921): 30–59.

Delegates of the Cherokee Nation. *Communication of the Delegates of the Cherokee Nation to the President of the United States, Submitting the Memorial of their National Council, with the Correspondence Between John Ross, Principal Chief, and Certain Officers of the Rebellious States*. Washington, D.C.: Government Printing Office, 1866.

Grayson, George Washington. *A Creek Warrior for the Confederacy: The Autobiography of Chief G. W. Grayson*. Edited by W. David Baird. Norman: University of Oklahoma Press, 1988.

Hitchcock, Ethan Allen. *A Traveler in Indian Territory: The Journal of Ethan Allen Hitchcock*. Edited by Grant Foreman. Norman: University of Oklahoma Press, 1930.

Kappler, Charles J., ed. *Indian Affairs: Laws and Treaties*. 5 vols. Washington, D.C.: Government Printing Office, 1904.

Lewis, Anna. "Diary of a Missionary to the Choctaws, 1860–1861." *Chronicles of Oklahoma* 17 (1939).

Moulton, Gary, ed. *The Papers of Chief John Ross, 1840–1866*. 2 vols. Norman: University of Oklahoma Press, 1985.

Rawick, George P., ed. *The American Slave: A Composite Autobiography*. 12 vols. Supplement series I, vol. 12. Westport, Conn.: Greenwood Press, 1977.

Richardson, James D., ed., *The Messages and Papers of Jefferson Davis and the Confederacy*. 2 vols. New York: Chelsea House, Robert Hector Publishers, 1966.

Royce, Charles. "The Cherokee Nation of Indians." *Fifth Annual Report of the Bureau of Ethnology*. Washington, D.C.: Government Printing Office, 1887.

U.S. War Department. *War of the Rebellion: A Compilation of the Official Records of the Union and Confederate Armies*. 128 vols. Washington, D.C.: Government Printing Office, 1880–1901.

NEWSPAPERS

Cherokee Advocate
Fort Smith Herald

BOOKS AND ARTICLES

Abel, Annie Heloise. *The American Indian as Slaveholder and Secessionist*. 1915. Reprint, Lincoln: University of Nebraska Press, 1992.

———. *The American Indian in the Civil War, 1862–1865*, originally published as *The American Indian as Participant in the Civil War*. Cleveland: Arthur Clark Company, 1919. Reprint, Lincoln: University of Nebraska Press, 1992.

———. *The American Indian and the End of the Confederacy, 1863–1866*. 1925. Reprint, Lincoln: University of Nebraska Press, 1993.

———. "The Indian in the Civil War." *American Historical Review* 15 (January 1910): 281–96.

Adair, James. *History of the American Indians*. Edited by Samuel Cole Williams. 1775. Reprint, Johnson City, Tenn.: Watauga Press, 1930.

Agnew, Brad. *Fort Gibson: Terminal of the Trail of Tears*. Norman: University of Oklahoma Press, 1980.

Anderson, William L., ed. *Cherokee Removal: Before and After*. Athens: University of Georgia Press, 1991.

Andrews, Thomas. "Freedmen in Indian Territory: A Post-Civil War Dilemma." *Journal of the West* 4 (1965): 367–76.

Ash, Stephen V. *When the Yankees Came: Conflict and Chaos in the Occupied South*. Chapel Hill: University of North Carolina Press, 1995.

Bahos, Charles. "On Opothleyahola's Trail: Locating the Battle of Round Mountain." *Chronicles of Oklahoma* 63 (Spring 1985): 58–89.

Bailey, M. Thomas. *Reconstruction in Indian Territory: A Story of Avarice, Discrimination, and Opportunism.* Port Washington, N.Y.: Kennikat Press, 1972.

Baird, W. David. *Peter Pitchlynn: Chief of the Choctaws.* Norman: University of Oklahoma Press, 1972.

Banks, Dean. "Civil War Refugees from Indian Territory in the North, 1861–1864." *Chronicles of Oklahoma* 41 (1963): 286–98.

Barton, Michael. *Goodmen: The Character of Civil War Soldiers.* University Park: Penn State Press, 1981.

Bass, Althea. *Cherokee Messenger.* Norman: University of Oklahoma Press, 1936.

Bearss, Edwin C. "The Civil War Comes to Indian Territory, 1861: The Flight of Opothleyahola." *Journal of the West* 11 (January 1972): 9–42.

Bearss, Edwin C., and Arrell M. Gibson. *Fort Smith: Little Gibraltar on the Arkansas.* Norman: University of Oklahoma Press, 1969.

Berkhofer, Richard. *Salvation and the Savage: An Analysis of Protestant Missions and American Indian Response, 1787–1862.* Louisville: University of Kentucky Press, 1965.

Berlin, Ira, et al. *Slaves No More, Three Essays on Emancipation and the Civil War.* New York: Cambridge University Press, 1992.

Braund, Kathryn E. Holland. *Deerskins and Duffels: The Creek Indian Trade with Anglo-America, 1685–1815.* Lincoln: University of Nebraska Press, 1993.

Britton, Wiley. *The Civil War on the Border, 1861–1862.* New York: G. P. Putnam's Sons, 1890.

———. *The Union Indian Brigade in the Civil War.* Kansas City, Mo.: Franklin Hudson Publishing Co., 1922.

Brown, Walter Lee. *A Life of Albert Pike.* Fayetteville: University of Arkansas Press, 1997.

Cantell, M. L., and Mac Harris, eds. *Kepis and Turkey Calls: An Anthology of the War Between the States in Indian Territory.* Oklahoma City: Oklahoma Historical Society, 1982.

Champagne, Duane. *American Indian Societies: Strategies and Conditions of Political and Cultural Survival.* Cambridge, Mass.: Cultural Survival Inc., 1989.

———. *Social Order and Political Change: Constitutional Governments among the Cherokee, the Choctaw, the Chickasaw, and the Creeks.* Stanford: Stanford University Press, 1992.

Clinton, Catherine. *The Other Civil War: American Women in the Nineteenth Century.* New York: Hill and Wang, 1984.

Coleman, Michael. *American Indian Children at School, 1850–1930.* Jackson: University Press of Mississippi, 1993.

Cottrell, Steve. *Civil War in the Indian Territory.* Gretna, La: Pelican, 1995.

Cunningham, Frank. *General Stand Watie's Confederate Indians.* San Antonio, Tex.: The Naylor Company, 1959.

Cutrer, Thomas W. *Ben McCulloch and the Frontier Military Tradition.* Chapel Hill: University of North Carolina Press, 1993.

Dale, Edward Everett. "The Cherokees in the Confederacy." *Journal of Southern History* 13 (May 1947): 160–85.

Danziger, Edmund J. *Indians and Bureaucrats: Administering the Reservation Policy During the Civil War.* Urbana: University of Illinois Press, 1974.

Danziger, Edward. "The Office of Indian Affairs and the Problem of Civil War Refugees in Kansas." *Kansas Historical Quarterly* 35 (Autumn 1969): 267–75.

Davis, William C. *The Cause Lost: Myths and Realities of the Confederacy.* Lawrence: University Press of Kansas, 1996.

Debo, Angie. *And Still the Waters Run.* Princeton, N.J.: Princeton University Press, 1940.

———. "The Location of the Battle of Round Mountain." *Chronicles of Oklahoma* 41 (Spring 1963): 70–104.

———. *The Rise and Fall of the Choctaw Republic.* Norman: University of Oklahoma Press, 1934.

———. *The Road to Disappearance.* Norman: University of Oklahoma Press, 1941.

———. "Southern Refugees of the Cherokee Nation." *Southwestern Historical Quarterly* 35 (April 1932): 255–66.

Degler, Carl. *The Other Side: Southern Dissenters in the Nineteenth Century.* New York: Harper and Row, 1974.

DeRosier, Jr., Arthur H. *The Removal of the Choctaw Indians.* Knoxville: University of Tennessee Press, 1970.

Doran, Michael. "Population Statistics of Nineteenth-Century Indian Territory." *Chronicles of Oklahoma* 53 (1975–76): 492–515.

DuChateau, Andre Paul. "The Creek Nation on the Eve of the Civil War." *Chronicles of Oklahoma* 52 (Fall 1974): 290–315.

Duncan, Robert Libscomb. *Reluctant General: The Life and Times of Albert Pike.* New York: Dutton, 1961.

Evans, E. Raymond. "Highways to Progress: Nineteenth Century Roads in the Cherokee Nation." *Journal of Cherokee Studies* 2 (Fall 1977): 394–400.

Faulk, Odie B., Kenny Franks, and Paul Lambert, eds. *Early Military Forts and Posts in Oklahoma.* Oklahoma City: Oklahoma Historical Society, 1978.

Faust, Drew Gilpin. *Mothers of Invention.* Chapel Hill: University of North Carolina Press, 1996.

Fehrenbacher, Donald. "The Missouri Controversy and the Source of Southern Separatism." *Southern Review* XIV (1978): 653–657.

Fellman, Michael. *Inside War: The Guerrilla Conflict in Missouri During the American Civil War.* New York: Oxford University Press, 1989.

Fischer, LeRoy, ed. *The Civil War Era in Indian Territory.* Los Angeles: Lorrin L. Morrison Publisher, 1974.

Fisher, LeRoy, and Jerry Gill. "Confederate Indian Forces Outside of Indian Territory." *Chronicles of Oklahoma* 46 (Fall 1968): 249–84.

Fisher, LeRoy, and Kenny A. Franks. "Confederate Victory at Chusto-Talasah." *Chronicles of Oklahoma* 49 (Winter 1971–72): 452–76.

Fisher, LeRoy and William McMurray, "Confederate Refugees From Indian Territory." *Chronicles of Oklahoma* 57 (Winter 1979–80): 451–462.

Foner, Eric. *Reconstruction: America's Unfinished Revolution, 1863–1877.* New York: Harper and Row, 1988.

Foreman, Carolyn. "John Jumper." *Chronicles of Oklahoma* 29 (Summer 1951): 137–52.

———. *Park Hill.* Muscogee, Okla.: Star Printery, 1948.

Foreman, Grant. *Indian Removal: The Emigration of the Five Civilized Tribes of Indians.* Norman: University of Oklahoma Press, 1932.

———. *The Five Civilized Tribes.* Norman: University of Oklahoma Press, 1934.

Foreman, Minta Ross. "Reverend Stephen Foreman: Cherokee Missionary." *Chronicles of Oklahoma* 18 (September 1940):229–42.

Franks, Kenny. *Stand Watie and the Agony of the Cherokee Nation.* Memphis: Memphis State University Press, 1979.

Franzmann, Tom. "The Final Campaign: The Confederate Offensive of 1864." *Chronicles of Oklahoma* 63 (Fall 1985): 26–79.

Gaines, W. Craig. *The Confederate Cherokees: John Drew's Regiment of Mounted Rifles.* Baton Rouge: Louisiana State University Press, 1989.

Gearing, Fred. *Priests and Warriors: The Social Structure of Cherokee Politics in the 18th Century.* Menasha, Wisc.: American Anthropological Society Memoir 93, 1962.

Gibson, Arrell M. *The Chickasaws.* Norman: University of Oklahoma Press, 1971.

Gibson, Ronald, ed. *Jefferson Davis and the Confederacy and Treaties Concluded by the Confederate States with the Indian Tribes.* Dobbs Ferry, N.Y.: Oceana Publications, 1977.

Glatthaar, Joseph. *Forged in Battle: The Civil War Alliance of Black Soldiers and White Officers.* New York: Meridian, 1991.

Grand Chapter of Royal Arch Masons of Oklahoma. *History of the Grand Chapter of the Royal Arch Masons of Oklahoma.* Oklahoma City, 1964.

Graves, William H. "Indian Soldiers for the Gray Army: Confederate Recruitment in Indian Territory." *Chronicles of Oklahoma* 69 (Summer 1991): 134–45.

Green, Michael. *The Politics of Indian Removal: Creek Government and Society in Crisis.* Lincoln: University of Nebraska Press, 1982.

Griffith, Benjamin. *McIntosh and Weatherford, Creek Indian Leaders.* Tuscaloosa: University of Alabama Press, 1988.

Hagan, William T. *American Indians.* Chicago: University of Chicago Press, 1961.

Hale, Douglas. "Rehearsal for Civil War: The Texas Cavalry in the Indian Territory, 1861." *Chronicles of Oklahoma* 68 (Summer 1990): 228–65.

Halliburton, R., Jr. *Red over Black: Black Slavery Among the Cherokee Indians.* Westport, Conn.: Greenwood Press, 1977.

Hammond, Sue. "Socioeconomic Reconstruction in the Cherokee Nation, 1865–1870." *Chronicles of Oklahoma* 56 (Summer 1978): 158–70.

Harriman, Helga. "Economic Conditions in the Creek Nation, 1865–1871." *Chronicles of Oklahoma* 51 (Fall 1973): 325–34.

Hauptman, Laurence M. *Between Two Fires: American Indians in the Civil War.* New York: The Free Press, 1995.

Heath, Gary N. "The First Federal Invasion of Indian Territory." *Chronicles of Oklahoma* 44 (Winter 1966–67): 409–19.

Hess, Earl J. and William L. Shea. *Pea Ridge: Civil War Campaign in the West.* Chapel Hill: University of North Carolina Press, 1992.

Hood, Fred. "Twilight of the Confederacy in the Indian Territory." *Chronicles of Oklahoma* 41 (Winter 1963–1964): 425–41.

Horton, Louise. *Samuel Bell Maxey: A Biography.* Austin: University of Texas Press, 1974.

Hudson, Charles. *The Southeastern Indians.* Knoxville: University of Tennessee Press, 1976.

Hutchins, John. "The Trial of Reverend Samuel A. Worcester." *Journal of Cherokee Studies* 2 (Fall 1977): 356–74.

James, Parthena Louise. "Reconstruction in the Chickasaw Nation: The Freedmen Problem." *Chronicles of Oklahoma* 45 (Spring 1967): 44–57.

Johnston, Carolyn Ross. *Cherokee Women in Crisis: Trail of Tears, Civil War, and Allotment, 1838–1907.* Tuscaloosa: University of Alabama Press, 2003.

Jordan, H. Glenn, and Thomas M. Holm, eds. *Indian Leaders: Oklahoma's First Statesmen.* Oklahoma City: Oklahoma Historical Society, 1979.

Josephy, Alvin. *500 Nations.* New York: Alfred Knopf, 1994.

Kensell, Lewis Anthony. "Phases of Reconstruction in the Choctaw Nation 1865–1870." *Chronicles of Oklahoma* 47 (Summer 1969): 138–53.

King, Duane, ed. *The Cherokee Indian Nation.* Knoxville: University of Tennessee Press, 1979.

Lancaster, Jane F. *Removal Aftershock: The Seminoles' Struggle to Survive in the West, 1836–1866.* Knoxville: University of Tennessee Press, 1994.

Lee, Keun Sang. "The Capture of the *J. R. Williams.*" *Chronicles of Oklahoma* 55 (Spring 1982): 22–33.

Littlefield, Daniel, Jr. *Africans and Creeks: From the Colonial Period to the Civil War.* Westport, Conn.: Greenwood Press, 1979.

———. *Africans and Seminoles: From Removal to Emancipation.* Westport, Conn.: Greenwood Press, 1977.

———. *The Cherokee Freedmen: From Emancipation to American Citizenship.* Westport, Conn.: Greenwood Press, 1978.

———. *The Chickasaw Freedmen: A People Without a Country.* Westport, Conn.: Greenwood Press, 1980.

McLoughlin, William. *After the Trail of Tears: The Cherokees' Struggle for Sovereignty, 1839–1880.* Chapel Hill: University of North Carolina Press, 1993.

———. *Champions of the Cherokees, Evan and John B. Jones.* Princeton. N.J.: Princeton University Press, 1990.

———. *The Cherokees and Christianity, 1794–1870, Essays on Acculturation and Cultural Persistence.* Edited by Walter H. Conser Jr. Athens: University of Georgia Press, 1994.

———. *Cherokee Renascence in the New Republic.* Princeton, N.J.: Princeton University Press, 1986.

———. "Red Indians, Black Slavery and White Racism: American Slaveholding Indians." *American Quarterly* 26 (October 1974): 367–85.

McNeal, Kenneth. "Confederate Treaties with the Tribes of Indian Territory." *Chronicles of Oklahoma* 42 (Winter 1964–65): 408–20.

McPherson, James M., ed. *The Atlas of the Civil War*. New York: MacMillan, 1994.

————. *Battle Cry of Freedom: The Civil War Era*. New York: Ballantine Books, 1988.

————. *For Cause and Comrades: Why Men Fought in the Civil War*. New York: Oxford University Press, 1997.

————. *The Negro's Civil War*. Urbana: University of Illinois Press, 1982.

McReynolds, Edwin C. *The Seminoles*. Norman: University of Oklahoma Press, 1957.

Martin, Joel. *Sacred Revolt: The Muscogee's Struggle for a New Order*. Boston: Beacon Press, 1991.

Massey, Mary Elizabeth. *Refugee Life in the Confederacy*. Baton Rouge: Louisiana State University Press, 1964.

May, Katja. *African Americans and Native Americans in the Creek and Cherokee Nations, 1830s to 1920s*. New York: Garland Publishing, 1996.

Meserve, John Bartlett. "Chief John Ross." *Chronicles of Oklahoma* 13 (December 1935): 421–37.

————. "Chief Opothleyahola." *Chronicles of Oklahoma* 9 (December 1931): 445–53.

Mihesuah, Devon A. *Cultivating the Rosebuds: The Education of Women at the Cherokee Female Seminary, 1851–1909*. Urbana: University of Illinois Press, 1993.

Miner, H. Craig. *The Corporation and the Indian: Tribal Sovereignty and Industrial Civilization in Indian Territory, 1865–1907*. Columbia: University of Missouri Press, 1976.

Mitchell, Reid. *Civil War Soldiers*. New York: Touchstone, 1988.

————. *The Vacant Chair: The Northern Soldier Leaves Home*. New York: Oxford University Press, 1993.

Monaghan, Jay. *Civil War on the Western Border, 1854–1865*. Lincoln: University of Nebraska Press, 1955.

Mooney, James. "Myths of the Cherokee," *19th Annual Report, Bureau of American Ethnology*. 1900. Reprint, Nashville: Charles and Randy Moore Elder Booksellers, 1982.

Moore, Francis M. *A Brief History of the Missionary Work in Indian Territory of the Indian Mission Conference, Methodist Episcopal Church South*. Muskogee, Indian Territory: Phoenix Printing Co., 1899.

Morris, John W., Charles R. Goins, and Edwin C. McReynolds. *Historical Atlas of Oklahoma*. Norman: University of Oklahoma Press, 1986.

Morton, Ohland. "Confederate Government Relations with the Five Civilized Tribes." *Chronicles of Oklahoma* 31 (1953): 189–204.

———. "Reconstruction in the Creek Nation." *Chronicles of Oklahoma* 9 (1931): 171–79.

Moulton, Gary. "John Ross and W. P. Dole: A Case Study of Lincoln's Federal Indian Policy." *Journal of the West* 12 (July 1977): 414–23.

———. *John Ross: Cherokee Chief.* Athens: University of Georgia Press, 1978.

Neilson, John C. "Indians, Masters, Black Slaves: An Oral History of the Civil War in Indian Territory." *Panhandle-Plains Historical Review* 65 (1922): 42–54.

Nichols, David A. *Lincoln and the Indians, Civil War Policy and Politics.* Columbia: University of Missouri Press, 1978.

O'Brien, Greg. *Choctaws in a Revolutionary Age, 1750–1830.* Lincoln: University of Nebraska Press, 2002.

Paludan, Phillip Shaw. *Victims: A True Story of the Civil War.* Knoxville: University of Tennessee Press, 1981.

———. *"A People's Contest": The Union and Civil War, 1861–1865.* New York: Harper and Row, 1988.

Perdue, Theda. "The Conflict Within: Cherokees and Removal." In *Cherokee Removal: Before and After,* edited by William Anderson, 55–74. Athens: University of Georgia Press, 1991.

Perdue, Theda, ed. *Cherokee Editor: The Writings of Elias Boudinot.* Knoxville: University of Tennessee Press, 1983.

———. *Cherokee Women: Gender and Cultural Change, 1700–1835.* Lincoln: University of Nebraska Press, 1998.

———. *"Mixed Blood" Indians: Racial Construction in the Early South.* Athens: University of Georgia Press, 2003.

———. *Slavery and the Evolution of Cherokee Society, 1540–1866.* Knoxville: University of Tennessee Press, 1979.

Rable, George. *Civil Wars: Women and the Crisis of Southern Nationalism.* Urbana: University of Illinois Press, 1989.

Rampp, Larry C., and Donald L. Rampp. *The Civil War in the Indian Territory.* Austin: University of Texas Press, 1975.

Ruff, Rowena McClinton. "Notable Persons in Cherokee History: Charles Hicks." *Journal of Cherokee Studies* 17: 16–27.

Saunt, Claudio. *A New Order of Things: Property, Power, and the Transformation of the Creek Indians, 1733–1816.* New York: Cambridge University Press, 1999.

Shirk, George H. "The Place of Indian Territory in the Command Structure of the Civil War." *Chronicles of Oklahoma* 45 (Winter 1967–68): 464–71.

Shoemaker, Arthur. "The Battle of Chustenahlah." *Chronicles of Oklahoma* 38 (Summer 1960): 180–84.

Smith, Jane F. and Robert Kvasnicka, eds. *Indian White Relations: A Persistent Paradox.* National Archives Conference on Research in the History of Indian White Relations. Washington, D.C.: Howard University Press, 1971.

Starr, Emmet. *History of the Cherokees and Their Legends and Folklore.* Oklahoma City: Warden, 1921.

Sturm, Circe. *Blood Politics: Race, Culture, and Identity in the Cherokee Nation of Oklahoma.* Berkeley: University of California Press, 2002.

Thoburn, Joseph, ed. "The Cherokee Question." *Chronicles of Oklahoma* 2 (June 1924): 141–252.

Thornton, Russell. *The Cherokees: A Population History.* Lincoln: University of Nebraska Press, 1990.

———. "Cherokee Population Loss During the Trail of Tears: A New Perspective." *Ethnohistory* 31, no. 4 (Autumn 1984): 289–300.

Trickett, Dean. "The Civil War in Indian Territory, 1861." *Chronicles of Oklahoma* 18 (June 1940): 266–80.

———. "The Civil War in Indian Territory, 1862." *Chronicles of Oklahoma* 19 (December 1941): 381–96.

Wallace, Anthony F. C. *The Long and Bitter Trail: Andrew Jackson and the Indians.* New York: Hill and Wang, 1993.

Warde, Mary Jane. *George Washington Grayson and the Creek Nation, 1843–1920.* Norman: University of Oklahoma Press, 1999.

———. "Now the Wolf Has Come: The Civilian War in Indian Territory." *Chronicles of Oklahoma* 71 (Spring 1993): 69–87.

Wardell, Morris L. *A Political History of the Cherokee Nation, 1838–1907.* Norman: University of Oklahoma Press, 1938.

Warren, Hannah. "Reconstruction in the Cherokee Nation." *Chronicles of Oklahoma* 45 (Summer 1967): 180–89

Waugh, John C. *Sam Bell Maxey and the Confederate Indians.* Fort Worth, Tex.: Ryan Place Publishers, 1995.

Whipple, Charles K. *Relation of the American Board of Commissioners for Foreign Missions to Slavery.* Boston: R. F. Wallcut, 1861.

White, Christine Schultz, and Benton R. White. *Now the Wolf Has Come: The Creek Nation in the Civil War.* College Station: Texas A&M University Press, 1996.

White, Richard. *Roots of Dependency: Subsistence, Environment, and Social Change Among the Choctaws, Pawnees, and Navajos.* Lincoln: University of Nebraska Press, 1983.

Wilson, T. Paul. "Delegates of the Five Civilized Tribes to the Confederate Congress." *Chronicles of Oklahoma* 53 (Fall 1975): 353–66.
Wilson, Walt. "Freedmen in Indian Territory During Reconstruction." *Chronicles of Oklahoma* 49 (Summer 1971): 230–44.
Woodward, Grace Steele. *The Cherokees.* Norman: University of Oklahoma Press, 1963.
Wright, J. Leitch, Jr. *Creeks and Seminoles: The Destruction and Regeneration of the Muscogulge People.* Lincoln: University of Nebraska Press, 1986.
Wright, Muriel, ed. "Notes on the Life of Mrs. Hannah Worcester Hicks and the Park Hill Press." *Chronicles of Oklahoma* 19 (December 1941): 348–55.

UNPUBLISHED MATERIALS

Bahos, Charles Lee. "John Ross: Unionist or Secessionist in 1861?" Master's thesis, University of Tulsa, 1968.
Barry, Neil. "Federal Ascendancy in Indian Territory, 1862–1863." Master's thesis, Oklahoma State University, 1966.
Gill, Jerry. "Federal Refugees from Indian Territory, 1861–1867." Master's thesis, Oklahoma State University, 1977.
Mayberry, Robert. "Texans and the Defense of the Confederate Northwest, April 1861–April 1862: A Social and Military History." Ph.D. diss., Texas Christian University, 1992.
Tyner, Howard. "The Keetoowah Society in Cherokee History." Master's thesis, University of Tulsa, 1949.

Index